wOnderlust

A collection of story essays on traveling, doubting, and learning to endlessly wonder.

AmyRose Tomlinson

outskirts
press

Outskirts Press, Inc.
http://www.outskirtspress.com

ISBN: 978-1-4787-7443-3

Outskirts Press and the "OP" logo are trademarks belonging to Outskirts Press, Inc.

PRINTED IN THE UNITED STATES OF AMERICA

Thanks

Amy, thank you for being the first to say you'd be reading my book one day—and for doing just that. Julie, thank you for reading and constantly asking for more. Justin, thank you for your time and your editing expertise. Abbie and Zachry, thank you for listening to my thoughts, my questions, my ramblings, my unbelief—and for loving and accepting me unconditionally. Fern, thank you for inspiration and courage—and for teaching me, through Miriam, to look outside myself.

Thank you for seeing me.

Lucas, thank you for not allowing me to ever grow up—and for reminding me constantly of how capable I am. Bri, thank you for allowing me to share your story and therefore playing a vital role in the journey of this book. Thank you for allowing me into your life. Thank you for your vulnerability. Bethany, thank you for allowing me to lead you, even when I feel entirely unworthy. Thank you for thinking I am wonderful, even when I feel so far from it. Thank you for kind words and for lifting me up. Trista, thank you for sharing your brokenness with me—your *life* rather. Thank you for allowing me to love you. To touch you. Thank you for your vulnerability. Thank you for what you told me in Korea. Thank-you Mrs. Pierros, Mr. Vass, Ms. Zavalia, Mrs. Keith, Dr. Hil-Standford, and Dr. Tappmeyer for both affirmation and literary guidance.

Mom and Dad, thank you for helping me to become the person I am today and for teaching me to always be a skeptic and to demand Truth. Thank you for teaching me the importance of Hope—and that a life without it is no life at all. Sara, thank you for always believing in me and my dreams, no matter how ridiculous or illogical they may seem to everyone else. Thank you for being my lifeboat.

Naks, thank you for countless hours of listening and feedback while sharing Sleepytime tea and ginger snaps in our Ugandan bedroom. Thank-you for endless encouragement and convincing me to follow through with this dream.

Nancy. Thank you for editing. For understanding. For simply knowing. Thank you for this book.

Whybecause

When I taught English as a second language in Korea, my kindergarten students often said something that never failed to bring a smile. They were storytellers. And when telling a story, they often included the word, "whybecause." I do not mean, "why?" followed by "because." They actually said, *whybecause.*

Example:

"AmyRose Teacher, yesterday, I went to Lotte Department store. Whybecause? I had to buy a new pair of shoes."

This is my *whybecause.* I wrote this book why? Because . . .

I think too often we assume we know more than we do of life, of religion, and mostly of God. I'm not convinced we are supposed to know, or even understand as much as we think we are. I think we were created to be creatures of wonder, not of omniscience. And I think it the most dangerous place we can come to when we cease to wonder, and instead accept all as is, fearing if we begin to question or wonder too deeply we may soon be consumed by doubt and fear.

Mostly what you hold in your hands are the random thoughts, experiences and hopefully even truths that I have come to know through various people and places. While I feel that most authors set out to write what they *know*, I have done just the opposite. I have written what I don't know—what we don't know—as Christians, as atheists, as Muslims, as Jews. But mostly just as human beings existing, seeking, questioning.

While I would like to promise you words of Hope and divine inspiration, I cannot do so. What I can promise you is raw candor. The uncomfortable kind. I can promise you entirely unedited thought.

When I first began writing this book, I believed it to be a sort of Christian inspirational manuscript. As I wrote I was working my way through reading the four Gospels repetitively. My writing was—religious—and my hope was to inspire a deeper faith. But somewhere through the journey of this book something entirely unexpected happened.

I lost my faith.

I know, it has become a quite cliché term that seems to have lost its potency and meaning entirely. I guess I can't say I lost my *faith*. I still believe—in people, in unconditional love—even in God. But I lost *my* faith. The inerrant, Jesus-was-the-product-of-a-virgin-birth-death-on-a-cross-Only-Way-to-heaven-faith. The faith that defined me.

I'm not entirely sure how it happened, but it did. Maybe it was a combination of living in a new place, working in a new environment, for once not being surrounded by fundie-evangelical free 'Christians.' Maybe it was due to my departure from my Baptist university, my Baptist church, my Baptist employer. Or perhaps at least a part of it can be attributed to the doubt and disbelief of a dear friend. One who brought me alongside him to a road of doubt and Fear, then left me alone with my disbelief.

But I am not convinced I have the right to blame any specific situation, any event, or any person. It seems such a loss is the sort of happening that is simply bound to be.

I will not tell you at this moment the outcome of my journey. Partially because I believe my journey is not yet over, just as yours is not. Faith, or lack thereof, is a journey in and of itself. It is not a split second in time. It is not in an instant that anyone can come to know God. It is a series of decisions, of choices, of love and loss and confusion and fear and hope. It is only throughout a desperate groping for the Truth that anyone can come to know even a fraction of who He is, and how we are to love.

What I will tell you is that the journey has been worth it. It continues to be. And the realizations I came to throughout the writing of this book will open your eyes and enliven your soul.

My hope is to invoke within you a spirit of *wonder*. I hope you never cease to wonder what is Truth and what is love and what is good. I hope you continue to wonder who God is—if

He is—and seek to find Him, not simply in the cathedrals, the mosques, the temples, the sanctuaries; but everywhere, in everything, in everyone. I hope you never cease to wonder where He is—and I hope your occasional wonder transforms into a constant state of *wOnderlust*.

Disclaimer

There are a few stories in this manuscript that are not true. They are realistic fiction based on completely true stories, but the way the stories are told in their entirety are not true. These stories will be *marked so you may know which ones are absolute truth and which are not.

Names have been changed. Almost all of them. So know that yes, in order to respect the privacy of the parties involved, almost all of the names throughout this book have been changed.

Although the book has been organized into sections according to where I lived at the time that I wrote them, there are a couple entries that are not necessarily chronologically correct. This is because they seemed to fit better with the theme of a different part of the book. But for the most part, if it is titled "Notes from Africa" it really was written in Africa.

Notes from Africa:

ON LOVING GOD

Eating Henrietta

Tonight I ate fried chicken that was not so much fried as it was still bleeding. Back in the States, partaking of fried chicken would be no big deal. A ten minute drive to the nearest KFC would render not only freshly battered, fried and greasy chicken, but also a choice of green beans, cole slaw, baked beans, or mashed potatoes on the side—not to mention a warm, moist and pre-buttered biscuit to boot.

In Entebbe, Uganda, however, this is not the case.

In Uganda it is common courtesy to get to know the chicken a bit before partaking of its meaty flesh. The chicken we ate tonight, I call her Henrietta, graced our presence a few days ago, when she was brought to our home as a gift. A small family living a few towns away from us had come to visit our dear JjaJja[1], and as an act of gratitude for her discipleship and service, they brought her a live chicken. Henrietta was a heavy-set, Caucasian chicken, fond of sitting under JjaJaja's mahogany

---

1 "JjaJja" means "grandmother" in Luganda, which is one of the 32 tribal languages of Uganda.

rocking chair, and also fond of relieving herself under it, as well as relieving herself in various other areas of our home. When I first met Henrietta, I was rather confused at her presence. Thoughts such as, *Why is there a chicken in our house? Where did this chicken come from? Will we have a pet chicken now? Is Henrietta capable of producing fresh eggs daily?* Crossed my mind. I quickly pulled my P.I.A.(Partner In Action) Stacie aside and asked her the obvious question:

"Have you ever watched that TV show, *House?*"

She had not.

I went on to explain how in one particular episode of the show a young man came in deathly ill, with some sort of fungus growing in his right hand. The fungus continued to spread until they eventually had to amputate his whole arm, the whole time unsure as to the cause of this deadly infection, which was slowly spreading to other limbs and extremities. Well, turned out he had some sort of chicken disease. I'm sure it wasn't actually called "chicken disease," but either way, he contracted whatever he had from one of the chickens he handled at the Cock Fights where he worked.

And here was Henrietta, making herself quite at home, relieving herself wherever she pleased, completely clueless to her nastiness and potential to kill us all, or at least be responsible for the amputation of our limbs.

I didn't know we would be eating fried chicken tonight. I was under the impression we would be eating cooked cabbage.

"Jimmy will be coming by later with the chicken. Be sure to watch for him," JjaJja said.

"Oh—the chicken is coming back? Where was she?" I innocently ask.

"The butcher," she matter of factly responded.

You can imagine the terror that suddenly filled my soul.

I ate Henrietta tonight.

She was still bleeding and very chewy and although I am far from a vegetarian and a lover of steak and chicken, eating Henrietta only days after I had met her face to face was a bit difficult for me. Something that was alive, that I watched and named and came to know—was dead. And not just dead, but brutally decapitated, plucked, cleaned, fried in hot grease and then devoured.

I wonder if Jesus ate chicken.

And I wonder if it was terribly difficult for Him to do so because he didn't just know the chicken from Mary's chicken coop, He actually *made* it. He constructed its genetic make-up, created its DNA strand by strand, decided the color of its feathers and the width of its beak and how many centimeters exactly between each claw and how many eggs it would produce in any given day and how many chickens it would have and how many pecking fights it would get into and the pitch and tone and volume of it's 'cluck'—and then He ate it. Or, He didn't. The Bible doesn't state that Jesus ate chicken. But it doesn't say He didn't either.

The thing about Jesus is we really don't know much about Him. We can say we know much because the Old Testament is full of prophecy about Jesus, and there are the four Gospels which are 100% Jesus, not to mention the rest of the Bible in its entirety which was written by God, as it was "God-breathed," and technically Jesus is God and God is Jesus so if Jesus/God wrote the Bible we must know quite a bit about Him.

But I don't really think so.

We don't know what His favorite color was, or where His favorite place to play as a child was. We don't know what the first thing He made as a carpenter was. We don't know what His first words were. We don't know what His first pet was or whether the first tree He climbed was a sycamore or a fig. We don't know if any of His playmates ever hurt his feelings or what they could have said to do so. We don't know if He preferred goat milk or water with his meals. We don't know many things.

There are many authors who write inspirational, factual things but we really know absolutely nothing about them. We know nothing except perhaps the "About the Author" flap on the sleeve of the book, telling us where he resides with his wife, three children, two dogs and one talking parrot in a small farm house in East Tennessee.

When it comes to knowing who Jesus really was, I think we were given the bare essentials. But I also think the bare essentials are enough, and that's why that's all we were given.

We were given just enough to believe; we were given Hope. I'm not trying to say we know nothing at all about Jesus or that He enjoys keeping us in the dark. What I'm saying is that Jesus *wants* us to know Him; He just purposefully didn't make it easy to get to know Him.

Think of it this way. . .

When a guy finds a girl that he really likes, the chase is half the glory. The pursuit, rather, is half the glory. I don't know that I've ever met a man who was perfectly content to win a girl's heart at the first attempt. Women who are more guarded and protective of their hearts are proven to be desirable. The reason these women are so cherished and adored once they do let the pursuer see their heart, is because it took time. And because he did not *truly* know her until they sat in their rockers in front of the fire place on Christmas Eve when all of the kids and grandkids and great grandkids were in bed, as they sat in complete and comfortable silence because nothing needed to be said because they already knew—this is why their love was good. I say 'good' and not 'great' or some other more intensely descriptive adjective, because when God made the world and us and He said, "This is good," so I figure 'good' is as good as it gets.

Their love was good because it wasn't instant.

It took time and nurturing, and seeking and yearning and desiring. Because to love is to act and can be done instantly, but to be *in love* is a state of being which takes quite a great deal of time and energy and commitment. And although I believe God calls us to *love* Him instantly, I believe the *falling in love* with Him takes a great deal of time.

And He wanted it that way. That is why we don't know if Jesus ate chicken. Because He didn't want us to know everything.

He wanted us to *wonder*; because it takes wondering to fall in love.

Adolf Hitler and Mountain Dew

Today I watched a man fall in love in no less than seven minutes. I am not the type who has ever believed in love at first sight, rather, lust at first sight. But I assure you, what I witnessed has changed my mind.

Seven minutes.

Stacie and I were sitting just outside our favorite shop owned by our newfound friend, a kind Ugandan man named Baka. We walked to Baka's just about every day, to sip iced cold Mountain Dew and Fanta Orange out of recycled glass bottles.

But today, our spot was taken. Today our once-so-welcoming nook complete with tree stump table and plastic chairs, was occupied by piles upon piles of boxes. Devastation set in quickly upon seeing such a site—but soon subsided upon realizing the table had been moved outside; where two benches sat on either side of our tree stump table. Perhaps this would do. Hesitant, we took a seat just outside of Baka's shop and began to sip away. And then it happened.

We were two young Caucasian women in Africa. *Of course* we were constantly noticed, constantly stared at, but rarely ever approached in such a way that was about to take place. Adolfo (I call him that because I do not know his name; and the most wretched, probably broken person I can think of is Adolf Hitler) approached Stacie, a fiery yet humble passion in his eyes:

"May I—May I seet?"

"May you what? Sit? Sure!"

I don't think Stacie believed in being uncordial to anyone ever. Adolfo proceeded to straddle the bench upon which Stacie sat, leaning forward anxiously, staring her dead in the eyes.

"You mind if—it is OK if I say—you are beautiful?"

Stacie laughs.

"No! No, I don't mind if you say I'm beautiful! Well, thank-you!"

She continues to suck on her straw. I, all the while sit across the table entirely entertained by the interaction I am witnessing.

"You have a number—I can call?"

"Ha ha ha. . .no. No I don't think so. I'm married. See my ring?"

"You are not."

"No—yes I really am. I have a ring—see? My husband is in the States. . ."

"I do not believe it. You have a certificate? Of marriage? Where?"

"Are you serious? Do people really carry certificates of marriage on their person at all times? I am married! I have a husband. I cannot be with you!"

The interrogation continued this way, back and forth for quite some time. It was quite humorous, really. Adolfo continued to question Stacie's credibility, refusing to believe she was married, while Stacie vehemently argued that she was, in fact, married to a young man back in the States.

It was humorous until I realized Adolfo was entirely serious. Stacie just reiterated for about the 13th time that she was, in fact, married, and it would absolutely not work out for Adolfo to also marry her.

Suddenly, he understood. For the first time during the conversation, all eye contact was lost; his gaze dropped in utter agony, and in the most hopeless and childlike voice he asked her,

"What will we *do*?"

Somehow, within that very last question, I realized the sincerity in poor Adolfo's voice.

He was devastated. Completely hopeless. He had found the woman he would marry, he was sure of it! And nothing could be done. Adolfo sat for a moment staring blankly at the littered street, then quickly removed himself from his pleading position on Stacie's bench and turned to walk inside Baka's shop.

Just as we thought the whole episode was over, Adolfo, with one foot already in the doorway, turned and looked longingly into Stacie's eyes, and whispered,

"I LOVE YOU."

And I believed him.

———•(◦)•———

Adolfo's love reminded me of middle school love, or first love. We all know of the cheerleader Heather who falls deeply in love with the quarter back Scott. It matters not that they have nothing in common except their rank in popularity. They were made for each other, they are sure. Despite parental warnings that 'high school relationships never last' the courtship continues, sometimes for weeks, maybe for all of freshman and sophomore year. She is the most breathtakingly beautiful thing he has ever seen. He is the man of her dreams, her knight in shining armor. The 'l-bomb' is dropped within a couple weeks, 'marriage' only days later.

This is love.

You know how the story goes. It doesn't. It ends. Nine times out of ten, it ends. Maybe Scott thought he may have gotten Heather pregnant, so he bails. Or maybe Heather and her family move states away due to her father's job relocation and the distance was too much to bear. Either way, it's over, and heartbreak ensues. Years, maybe decades and maybe only months down the road, both come to the same conclusion.

"Oh, I've never *really* been in love."

This realization, of course, only comes once she finds someone she truly does love in a mature and realistic way. Someone she will spend her life with, bear many children with, and enjoy until her dying days.

As ridiculous and pointless perhaps as her dearest Scott now seems to her, in those moments they were together, in the naïve and blind, reckless ways of the two, it was love. It was love then. As shallow as it may seem in hind's sight, as immature and childish, to the 16-year old romantic who knew no better and could see none other—it *was* love.

Such was the case of our dear Adolfo. He knew no different. So to him, Stacie really was love. And the pain swelling from his crushed heart could be seen in his broken eyes. Adolfo's love was childlike and innocent much like Heather and Scott's. They knew no better. They only believed with their whole hearts they were in love. Naïve love.

Reckless love.

I wonder what our faith would look like if we loved that way. Recklessly.

A dear friend of mine and former college roommate used to say the thing she admired most about me was my 'ability to love with reckless abandon.' It took me a while to understand what that really meant, but when I did it became probably the most meaningful thing she or anyone has ever said of me.

What if I loved God that way?

When Jesus talked about the greatest faith a man could have, the most humble, the most welcoming, the most precious in the Kingdom, He talked about children. He said that we should believe as they do—blindly. And the thing about kids is, they don't just have this amazing 'childlike faith' Jesus talks about. They love with reckless abandon. They see no faults. They have no doubts. They only believe.

They only love.

A child sees his mother give him food, sustaining his life, and so he loves her. It is only logical. A young girl sees her father fixing the family's broken down station wagon, which is seemingly beyond repair. He fixes what is broken, and so she loves him. No questions asked.

I wish I could love God that way.

I wish I could see that He fixed me when I was seemingly beyond repair. That He sustains my life. And so, no questions asked, I love Him. No doubts, no insecurities, just child-like love. I want to see Him as Adolfo saw Stacie; because that is how He sees me. He saw me and said, "You are beautiful." He was instantly in love at first sight. He saw absolutely no other way but to have me, all for Himself. But I had another love. I was taken, accounted for; I was the lover and wife of Self. Upon realizing I could not be called His in such a state, and with complete heartbreak in His voice, He said,

"What will we *do*?"

So He sent His son. The sacrifice of His one and only beloved and blameless Son is what it would take for Him to have me, for me to be His and only His. To be promised to sin no longer. And His last words were just as Adolfo's –faint, yet fierce,

"I LOVE YOU."

He uttered in His dying breath, "It is finished.

It is complete. I have won her. She is mine. To love and enjoy for all of eternity. *I love her.* If only she would love me in return.[2]*

---

2   * The "Notes from Africa" were written at a different time and in entirely different setting than the "Notes from America" and "Notes from Korea." Beliefs, convictions and worldviews were greatly changed and molded throughout the writing of this book, so it is important to note that some ideas and statements may seem contradictory to the writer's voice later in the book.

Paul in the Gutter

This morning I was reading in Acts about the persecution of Paul. I read how he was shuffled from city to city, judge to judge, ultimately just awaiting his eventual martyrdom. I read about the countless times Paul was beaten and chased by angry mobs, and at one point a fight became so violent, the commander feared that Paul might be *torn apart* by them, and ordered troops to go down, "rescue him from them, and bring him into the barracks."[3] So basically, there was some pretty intense argumentation going on. So intense, that Paul was in danger of being torn apart.

As I was reading this passage this morning, and wanting so badly to have some sort of instant, deep revelation about Paul or persecution, I soon became disappointed. I became disappointed because not only was my desire for instant scriptural revelation not granted, but I was having trouble sympathizing with Paul. Paul was being 'persecuted.' He was beaten, flogged, imprisoned, etc, on more than one occasion. And yes, it is all

---

3   Acts 23:10

quite sad. But really? Paul was once a persecutor of Christ himself. You reap what you sow, right?

Paul was simply reaping what he had sown. He threw rocks at Christians, so Jews threw rocks at him. I realize because of God's direct intervention in his life, former Saul had a total change of heart. I also realize Paul is quite possibly one of the most influential Christ-followers in all of history. I am not saying I dislike the guy. I am not saying he deserved what he got. What I am saying, is that until today I was just really having trouble feeling for him.

———————

I have a friend who, while reading the story of Jacob, Leah and Rachel aloud to me, began crying. She was not crying because of hormones, or because there had been a recent death in the family or break-up and Old Testament stories just really hit a nerve. She was tearing up over this ancient love story because to her, it wasn't just a story. It was real. And she explained to me that for the first time she had begun to read these Old Testament stories not as simply stories, but as real accounts of real people.

This is how I wanted so desperately to see Paul. I wanted to see him as a real person. I wanted to step back in time for just a moment, and be there as he was brutally beaten for his Savior's name. I wanted to know how it felt to watch, firsthand, a dear friend be mercilessly beaten, thrown about, trampled upon so badly that he was removed because "he might be torn apart by men." This morning I read of Paul's persecution and beatings by mobs of violently angry men, and I wished I could understand. I wished I could have seen it happen. I wished I were there.

This afternoon I very regrettably got precisely what I had asked for.

While riding in a more-than-full Ugandan taxi-van headed back towards Entebbe, the driver made an unusually long stop. Taxi-drivers are all about business, and are so quick to get back on the road and on towards their next customer they will start driving off before their co-worker has even a single foot inside the vehicle. But today our driver wasn't so quick to take off. Today the door-caddy was all the way in the van, door closed, ready to go, and the driver didn't make a move. His eyes were glued right where everyone else's were—to the man in the gutter, across the street, surrounded by and being brutally beaten by 10 Ugandan men. When I say "everyone's eyes" I don't mean just everyone within our van. I mean everyone who was in plain sight of this man.

And here is the sick part.

As we strained our necks to see, two Ugandan policemen approached the scene. My heart leapt; there was hope for this man.

And then it sank, as they walked away.

I turned to my Ugandan friend, Ivan, eyes bulging, heart racing in panic, and questioned, "Why did the police leave? Aren't they going to help him!?"

"No," he calmly responded. "The man is a thief. If you are a thief who gets caught you will be beaten to death."

I didn't know this man. I had never seen him, much less made his acquaintance; but I felt for him. As I and every other Ugandan in sight watched this man be stripped, dragged, and beaten to death, I ached for him. There's something about seeing a human soul utterly helpless, tormented, slowly ripped to shreds that hits a nerve in the human conscious. That morning I read about Paul and longed to witness his persecution, and that afternoon I saw him, in the gutters of Entebbe, "being torn apart by men."

I wanted to rescue 'Paul.' I wanted to jump out of the taxi, dodging the crazy drivers while sprinting across the street. I wanted to pluck the brutes off of this poor man. I didn't care if he was a thief. I wouldn't have cared if he was a murderer. The scene was appalling; it was completely inhumane, and unacceptable.

And all this got me to thinking, am I this passionate and ready-to-rescue those who are daily beaten around me?

Perhaps I do not witness a man being mercilessly beaten to death *physically* on a daily basis; but I do see those who are emotionally and spiritually beaten almost to death on a minute-by-minute basis. I see a co-worker so devastated over the loss of a loved one he can barley function. Yet my heart does not ache for him. I do not pour into the teenage girl who is beaten as well. She who was raped by her step-father and still bears the scars. She who is so familiar with death she barely recognizes life. I do not watch, mouth agape, in utter panic, when I see a weary homeless man with empty eyes.

I have longed so desperately to see Paul. To witness his mal-treatment. Yet I have failed to recognize that Paul is not limited to the thief in the gutters. The beating isn't always physical, and it isn't always by ten angry men. But it is always visible; the re-sult is always devastating. It is happening daily, before my eyes.

And the beating continues. The poor soul is stripped—of Truth, of identity, of dignity.

I look on. Others look on—Christ-followers look on. We wit-ness firsthand the persecution of Paul, and speak not, act not, lest we be injured ourselves during the course of action. And we surely cannot afford such a risk—to be personally harmed—potentially beaten . . . all simply for the name of Christ, and the sake of others.

Religious

"I like your Christ. I do not like your Christians.
Your Christians are so unlike your Christ."

-Gandhi-

The more I write, the more I come to realize I am lost. I am more lost and wandering and wondering than I ever knew I could be. I have read more books during my stay here in Africa than I did in all of high school and college combined (thank goodness for Spark Notes). In all my reading I have noticed a common theme, or idea, or perhaps even a Truth.

I have noticed that every Christian-authored book I have read seems to emphasize the fact that Christianity is about relationship rather than religion. When locals here ask why I have come to Africa, I tell them I am here to love on orphans and share Jesus' love with them and anyone else He brings into our path. A common response to this is:

"Oh, so you're religious."

I despise that term.

Religious. It makes me think of the Ten Commandments and blood sacrifices and rosaries and popes and calls to prayer five times a day and fancy buildings with expensive lighting and artsy bulletins.

It makes me think of 'Christians.' And I'm not so sure I want that label anymore. I know I don't want to be 'religious.' But I am beginning to wonder if I want to be 'Christian' either.

I don't want to sing, "You're all I want"[4] when I don't mean it. You're not all I want. I want more than You. I want better clothes and a steady income. I want someone to pay off my school loans so I am free to travel and write and do humanitarian aid projects without the constant worry of capitalized interest and debt. I want to go to coffee shops every day and sip on white chocolate mochas and dirty chais and caramel macciatos while I journal my heart out. I want to go to India to touch the lepers like You did. I want to make my little sister whole again. I want to write a bestseller. I want a flash for my camera. I want a car that my dad doesn't have to rebuild every other summer so it runs on all 4 cylinders. I want an American bed to sleep on. I want milk that doesn't taste like a cow smells. I want to be confident in myself and my abilities. I want to never struggle with cutting or depression again. I want to be liked, and to be desired. I want to be recognized. I want to really know it is

---

4   "You're All I want" is a Christian 'worship' often song sung in contemporary Christian worship gathering. The song lyrics basically say "You're all I want, You're all I need, You're all I ever want to be. . . .".

okay that I am not married or engaged or planning a wedding. That I am not abnormal because I am almost 25 and happy to be single and uncommitted.

I want so much. I want so much more than You.

I don't want to separate the holy from the unholy anymore. I want everything to be holy. I want to taste You when I eat my French toast smothered in peanut butter, syrup and sweet bananas. And when I eat my favorite 'Red Label' South African lemon cookies. When I drink I want to recognize it is You who is quenching my thirst—with Kenyan coffee or filtered water or Fanta Orange or white zin. I want to see You in the beggar's eyes. And in the sunrise over Lake Victoria. But also in the mangy half-starved mutts and diseased storks. When I walk the red dirt roads I want to feel You beneath my feet. And in the prostitute's embrace. And in the heat of the African sun beating down on my now leathery shoulders. I want to smell You in the first slice into a fresh pineapple. And also in the stench of the overflowing dumpsters in Kitoro. And in the armpits of joy-filled orphans who have not yet bathed. I want to hear you at night through the howling guard dogs, and in the morning when the neighbor child laughs and screams. I want to hear You even through the Ugandan men's constant lewd and inappropriate daily remarks.

And as I taste and see and feel and smell and hear You, I want to do so in worship. I want every act and every joy and every sorrow to be an act of worship to You. I want to enjoy You and recognize You, and admire You when I am breathing and thinking and eating and tasting and walking and listening and touching. I want to know how it is to live this way—to live in a constant state of worship and adoration—of a God I have come to know I do not know at all. . .but with whom I want so desperately to fall madly in love.[5]*

---

* Journal entry written in Uganda, East Africa, 2009.

Elias

Today was the worse clinic day ever[6]. We were all exhausted and the whole day was chaos.

But then I met Elias.

He was the 7lb. 8-month-old, incredibly malnourished son of a mother who sneaked into the clinic without our knowledge. The only reason I even noticed her to begin with was because she was sitting on one of our pharmacy benches. My usual instantaneous reaction would have been to throw her out or at least put her in the back of the line since she had no intake papers. I tried asking her if she had seen the doctor yet, or if she had papers, which she did not. I soon realized that she did not speak any English or Luganda—only Ki-Swahili.

I knelt down after noticing she had a baby in her arms and began to uncover him. That's when I realized why He showed her to me.

---

6   During my stay in Uganda I participated in a 10-day mobile medical clinic that served to travel throughout northeastern Uganda offering medical treatment to villages in the bush who would otherwise never have medical treatment of any kind.

I got a hold of Karen and Dottie and showed them the situation, and also grabbed John as I noticed the black bands on the babies' wrists.[7] While the ladies fed Elias oral rehydration solution thru a dropper, John and I prayed with the mother and child.

Later I went with Dan to get sugar, rice, beans, posho and oil for the family, and Dottie, Christina, Sharon and I took them home in our van. Home to a shack the size of our guest house bathroom in Entebbe. We brought them home in silence and rode back in tears, knowing regardless of our efforts, Elias would be lucky to last longer than a few more days. I was on emotional overload on the way back to the hotel.

But then we pulled up to the party.

It was Mama's birthday and Ugandans know how to celebrate. Music blasting, feast laid out, cake complete with candles and sparklers atop burning. And after the feast we had a dance party. Quite possibly the best dance party I've ever been a part of. Maybe because of the variety of attendees. Pastors, teachers, mothers, fathers, Americans, Ugandans, Kenyans, Egyptians, Mexicans. We danced the night away and, for a few hours, I forgot about Elias.

I forgot about Elias and the hundreds of locals waiting patiently outside our clinic doors without food or water, directly under the merciless African sun. I forgot about the HIV/AIDS victim whose entire body was covered in white, scaly skin. I forgot about his sad yellow eyes staring back at me as I handed him a pack of 30 multi-vitamins and sent him on his way. I forgot

---

7   Black bands are given by witch-doctors to those who seek their services

about the woman on the mat clawing at the cement ground with her barely-there nails, begging for help shortly before she guzzled an entire bottle of water I gave her in *one swallow*. I forgot about the emaciated young girl waiting on stage on the mat, in her bright white dress, calmly chewing on chipati and drinking cup after cup of water I poured her as she waited to be released after learning she had sickle-cell anemia.

And this morning as I sit and wait to leave for our next clinic site, I wonder how long, or not-so-long, it will take for me to forget the people I meet today. I wonder if a two-hour dance party enables me to forget the events of a day what an 18-hour plane ride back to the States where my home and all those dear to me will allow me to forget.

And I wonder if God ever forgets. Does He forget pain and suffering and sickness and hopelessness?

If he remembered every single tear that fell I think he may have to create a whole other planet just to contain them all. I don't think He holds on to them so He can dispense of them. I think He keeps them so He can remember how His children ached. So that when He sees us do things like break into a clinic and lie about being in line and cheat the system and those who've been waiting for nine hours straight without food or water— He has compassion on us.

And He moves my feet towards the woman on the bench with 7lb. 8-month-old Elias and whispers "LOVE" deep into my soul.

Muhumuza

In Uganda, children are given two first names. One is English and one is Ugandan. Shortly after my arrival in Uganda, I was graciously given a Ugandan name by a now dear friend, Katherine Bodo. She called me "Muhumuza", meaning "Comfort."

Yesterday[8] when traveling in a mini-van taxi packed with 19 other fellow-travelers on our way to Kampala from Jinja—I began contemplating the meaning of my Ugandan name, "Comfort." To be honest, I did not think it was at all fitting. Now give me a name that translates "Impulsive," or "Crazy" or "Stone Wall" or "I Have a Heart Deep Down, You'll Never See It, but One Day, Possibly, You'll Know I Care" any of these names would fit like a glove. But "Comfort"? Not so much. As far as I knew I was anything but Comforting. Only people like Mother Theresa or the nurturing, motherly type should be given a name meaning Comfort.

---

8   These are "notes"/journal entries written while living in Uganda, East Africa.

But not I.

The thing about travelling by taxi in Uganda is that you're guaranteed a whole lot of time to think, as a destination 5 miles away will take at least 30 minutes to get to, due to stopping every five yards to pick up yet another handful of passengers which there is clearly no room for, but who pile in anyway. So as we putted along in the taxi-van, jam-packed with quite the variety of travelers: a few young men, some Christians, some Muslims, some atheists, a hen, and a baby suckling his mother's bare breast, I began to ponder the events of the day.

Sitting four-wide in a back seat made for three, in the heat of Africa, with no a/c. Inhaling black smoke from the muffler just ahead of us that had clearly never been through any sort of emissions. Arriving to our destination about three hours early. Spending the afternoon staring at about 30 Ugandan widows who had all gathered together for a meeting with Agatha (whom we were waiting on) and did not realize she would not be arriving until about 3 hours later. Attempting to speak to the women through our dear friend and translator Ivan, but soon learning not one but six different tribal languages were spoken by these women.

Sitting in awkward silence.

All 30 women plus my crew of three plus a few staff piling into the medical center, into a room that happened to be about the size of our bedroom due to rain. Again, awkward silence. Waiting for the arrival of Agatha and husband. Final arrival and speeches and introductions, ceasing of rain. Tour of the slums of Jinja. Fresh, red, clay-like African mud. Lots of mud. Seeing the shacks the widows lived in with their 10 children and grandchildren. Shacks the size of your average American walk-in-closet. The smell of fish and grime and being covered in mud. Stopping at Agatha and Ronald's home on the way back where Ronald proceeded to spilled boiling hot Ugandan tea all over my blistered and bloodied and scabbed over feet.

And then the taxi ride home;
In the traffic.
And the stench.
And the tight quarters in which we sat.

And as I pondered all of these things, how uncomfortable the day was in the rain and the waiting and the mud and the cramped quarters and the boiling tea on my blistered feet—the most unsettling of realizations crossed my mind.

"Muhumuza."

Comfort.

Suddenly I understood. I don't think when God gave me this Ugandan name, He meant it as a confirmation that I am one who comforts. I think it was intended more as a self-fulfilling prophecy. In psychology we studied the labeling theory, in which people tend to become, or live up to, the label which they are given. For example; if someone from a very young age is told by their mother they are lazy, and that is the idea drilled into their minds, then eventually, that child will grow into the label he is given. He will probably become lazy, not realizing that is not what he was made for or intended to be, but that is what he was named, that is how he was labeled, so that is who he has become.

I realized that *Comfort* is who I had become. What I had become. Not since being in Uganda, but since the beginning. From the time I was birthed into my comfortable American life, in my comfortable four-bedroom home in my comfortable, purely Caucasian, American suburb, attending my comfortable Christian school kindergarten through college, working in a comfortable environment surrounded by Christians in New Orleans to working in a comfortable environment surrounded by Christians at the Missouri Baptist Children's Home—I had *become* Comfort.

That is who I was. Always comfortable. Always Comfort.

But in Uganda—there is heat and the rain and a plethora of unwanted insects. I have killed 29 bed bugs since my arrival. I have heard more kissing noises, marriage proposals, lewd comments and stares in the past six weeks than I have in my entire life. The beef sucks. There is no Sonic. There is no cheese, and so there are no cheeseburgers. I have to *walk* to the internet café and *pay* for the internet, which by the way, has worked only about 35% of the time.

I also walk to the market.
And the store.
And the church.
And the orphanage.
And the post office.

And I love walking. This would not be a problem at all except that I currently have seven very painful and open sores on my left foot due to broken or too small, or ill-fitting, cheap African shoes. My high E-string broke within the first week of our arrival. Strings here cost $50 rather than $7. My shoes broke. I duct-taped them back together, several times. And they continued to break. My sunglasses broke. My brand new Nikon camera purchased specifically for the trip broke. Our phone has decided to only work when people call for Stacie, and ceases working altogether when anyone calls for me. I don't sleep at night. I am exhausted all day. There are nineteen mosquito corpses on my mosquito net right now, and ZERO on Stacie's, due solely to the fact that mosquitoes apparently prefer brunettes. I'm sick of being surrounded by inappropriately staring people. I long to be surrounded by English speaking, Americans. I long for a Sonic cheeseburger. And a 44oz. cherry coke *with ice.*

I long for the *comfort* I have left behind. And am sickened upon realizing I have become the name I was given.

"Oh, my child," God has said, "When will you come to know, you cannot turn to comfort others, until *your* sole comfort is found in Me."

A Love Affair

Sometimes I think remembering a missed place is comparable to missing a lost lover. When one sits alone on his front porch pondering life and most especially his lonely state of being more than likely he will begin to remember, and long for his most recent special someone. When missing and longing, however, one tends only to remember the good. The way she smelled, the way he touched, the way she smiled. Nevermind the hurtful words still now resonating in one's mind, or the misery brought upon one another, regardless of being 'in love.'

This is how I see Africa. Like an ex-lover.

I chose to remember the warm days and the comfortably cool evenings. I remembered how the pineapple was so sweet and inexpressibly delicious I ate it every day until I had seven sores in my mouth all at once. I remembered how plentiful and tasty the avacodos were at only $0.25 a piece. I remembered how refreshing was the taste of an ice cold Fanta Orange from a glass bottle, being sipped through a straw while sitting just outside

Baka's shop in Entebbe town. I remembered how excited Baka was every time Stacie and I came to see him and how grateful we were that he never asked us for anything. I remembered the most beautiful sunrise I had ever seen on the shores of Lake Victoria. I remembered, most of all, the smiles and open arms of the Abba Home orphanage children and how thrilled they always were to see us—running full speed toward us every time we came to the home.

And what did I choose to forget?

I forgot how unbearable ice-cold squatty-baths are when covered in red grime. I forgot that literally every dog in the entire village would howl at the top of his lungs at 2:30am every morning and that at 3:30am the rooster would begin crowing in fifteen-second intervals for the next three hours straight. I forgot how cold are the stares of Ugandan women who are sure I am here only to steal their men. I failed to remember how unwelcoming can be the cockroaches covering the floor of the bathroom during my midnight toilet-run. I forgot how lonely and hostile is the walk on Wavah Road to the orphanage when I am alone—the stares and mutterings and constant cries of "Mzungu[9]! Mzungu! You give me your money!" I did not remember frequent power outages, or the greed and ungratefulness even of those I hold most near to my heart. I forgot that Uganda never sleeps—whether howling dogs or crowing cocks or boda-bodas[10] making midnight runs or children screaming—constant, incessant, *noise*.

---

9   Meaning, "white person"
10   moped/motorcycle taxis

I failed to remember these things because I *longed* for Africa. She was like a lost lover and all I could think to do was return to her embrace[11]. And upon arriving, was reminded of the coldness thereof. And though my heart the last two days has seemed to harden towards the broken place, it was taken yet again today when I saw the people gathered while thanking, celebrating, feasting. And mostly when my Abba[12] children never ceased smiling when they saw my face.

Today I was humbled. Reminded I should expect no recognition. That when I give, when I love, it should be done recklessly, and expecting nothing in return—only hoping, rather, that God's presence and goodness be made known.

I wonder if we are to God what Africa has become to me—a lost lover.

I wonder if He chooses to remember only the good, and then longs for our embrace. I wonder if that is why He continues to love us, cherish us, bless us abundantly when we ungratefully and continuously take, greedy and wanting.

But still we are remembered only for goodness, and we are loved anyway.

---

11   This journal entry was written during my return trip to Africa a year after returning to the States from my six-month stay.

12   Abba Home is the name of the orphanage my partner and I volunteered for and worked alongside during our stay in Uganda.

Hide & Seek

I think people imagine that God is playing a sort of eternal game of Hide & Seek with all of humanity. Like He is hiding around the corner with a cheesy grin on His face waiting for us to sing the right song or pray the right way or be in just the right spiritual mindset. I've heard that 'God can't be manipulated . . .He'll show up in His own timing. . .' While the idea is good that God's presence and voice is not under our control, I'm not entirely sure I agree with the concept.

I don't think God ever 'shows up.' I think He never left to begin with.

God is not hiding around the corner or across the street or far off in another galaxy. He is here—always here and always speaking. We are a blind and ignorant people who seem to believe God is most real, most evident, within the walls of a church building or the waters of a baptismal. Or perhaps on a mountaintop on a lone hike, surrounded by the beauty of creation. We believe His presence is dependent upon our personal spiritual state of being, that His Spirit will not reveal itself unless we are falling on the ground in unison pleading He come near. We assume He is waiting for a right action, a specific word, a change of heart.

Who was it that decided some things, some moments, some places, are spiritual and some are not?

Whoever it was has robbed us of a euphoric spiritual experience. He has robbed us of a euphorically spiritual life.

It seems the Spirit of God is more evident in the places the traditional church warns us never to be. I have felt more alive, more spiritually aware, in the arms of a Ugandan prostitute than I ever have while kneeling on a pew or singing a repetitive 'worship' song. To say 'God will show up when He pleases' is to me, entirely misleading.

He is here.

And He is not waiting to reveal Himself. He is not waiting to appear.

He is waiting for *us* to show up—to become aware—and to finally begin to recognize His constant presence and the reality of His Spirit everywhere, in everything, in everyone. He is whispering constantly into our desperate souls,

"I am here."

Braveheart Love-making

I once travelled with my alma mater to a small village just outside of San Salvador, El Salvador. We made up two teams which would, tentatively, have two wells drilled by the end of our eight-day visit. The villagers had no access to clean water, which meant all sorts of blood-bourne diseases eventually leading to death. We were there to drill wells, as well as give lessons on hygiene (such as don't prepare your dinner right next to the chicken poo). We would also be doing some child evangelism, sharing the story of Jesus Christ. It was a pretty fantastic setup, really. At the dedication of the well, the entire village would gather around while our team leader delivered the gospel message. A plaque was placed on the foundation of the well stating that Living Water International had provided material water, but Jesus Christ would provide *eternal* water, in order that they never thirst again. The whole trip was a great idea. Clean water, eternal Water, not to mention adorable El Salvadorian children, re-learning a little Spanish, and staying in a compound virtually on the shores of the Atlantic Ocean. It really could not have been any better.

But I remember being entirely frustrated during that trip. My boyfriend at the time had also come on the trip, and in a feeble attempt to 'stay focused on God and the task at hand,' we not only asked that we be put on separate drilling teams, but I basically ignored his existence altogether. Our team leader/mentor/ second 2nd father, affectionately known as "Papa Kurt" kindly pulled us aside one evening:

"You're trying way too hard. It's a beautiful night. Go for a walk on the beach. . .Enjoy each other's presence."

And so, because Papa Kurt was pretty much the ultimate authority in our lives second only to God, we did just as we were told. We went to have our romantic walk on the beach, under the stars, on a crisp spring night, the salty breeze from the ocean before us softly blowing against our sun-burnt cheeks—you get the point. It was a beautifully romantic setting.

Our walk began with small-talk about the trip. We talked of the wonderful weather and atmosphere. We were "enjoying each other's presence" as instructed, holding hands, kissing every now and then, you know, the things you most definitely cannot do in the view of the public eye while on a mission trip with an ultimately conservative Baptist university. We hadn't been walking far when we both spotted a rather large log, the remains of a palm tree, neatly set against an old wooden fishing boat. How quaint.

We took a seat.

The conversation portion of our talk did not last much

longer—we sat and stared at the stars, and then began to pray. To be honest, I don't remember what we prayed for specifically. I just remember it was horrid. Perhaps it sounds a bit blasphemous that I just referred to a conversation with God as 'horrid,' but let's not forget, I promised candor, not spiritual perfection. Perhaps the actual conversation in itself was not what was so terrible, rather it was my own personal feelings and emotions.

I prayed first. I like to do that when in a group of two or more because then I have no one to compare myself to. Then my prayer doesn't have to be as long as Julie's or as intimate as Wendy's or as spiritual as Rob's. You know, because apparently the better you are at praying out loud and the more biblical terms and theological phrases you use and also the voice inflexion and loudness—all of these seem to determine how good of a Christian you are or aren't.

So I prayed first. Then he prayed. Really I don't like to even use the term "pray" when I refer to what I witnessed that night. The word "pray" makes me think of a family with young children gathered around a dinner table, eyes squeezed shut, hands clasped, "God is good, God is great. . ." or for that matter, adults sitting around a dinner table doing pretty much the same thing, but in a more mature fashion and with more eloquent words.

So Thomas didn't really 'pray' next. He *conversed.* If you have ever walked in on your parents making love as kid, or if you haven't and you can imagine how dreadfully awful it would be, because you felt as if you were the intruder of the most private and intimate thing known to man, that is how sitting next to

Thomas on our palm tree log on the beach while he conversed
with God felt.

And not just an intruder like a first grade boy sneaking into
the little girls' restroom intruder either—the walking in on the
love-making of Braveheart William Wallace and his new young
bride in the forest only days before her throat is slit type of
intrusion. That's what this was.

At first I sat in reverence, head bowed, listening to his kind
words to His Savior. But as this holy conversation continued,
I began to feel more and more awkwardness in the situation. I
began to feel increasingly less comfortable. And as tears slowly
dripped down his reddened nose and cheeks, and his conversation became cries of longing and desperation, I realized he was
in love. My bow became a stare, which turned into a looking
to the heavens and then back to Thomas and then back to the
heavens and wondering at God, whisper-yelling at God,

"Where *are* You??!?!"

Eventually I left our palm tree log. In quite a hurry, I might
add.

I was an intruder.

This was not a man praying as the tax collector, in front of
a multitude yearning to be seen and heard by men. This was
a man who was deeply and intimately enthralled by his Lord
and Savior, broken in His presence. I wonder who was most
like that in the Bible. And I think it may have been David. I

don't know of anywhere in scripture where a man is actually weeping because of the presence of the Lord and the brokenness of his spirit, but I do know David 'cried out' to God often and also said that "A broken and contrite heart is what [God] desires." And now that I think about it, there was also Mary, who washed Jesus' feet with her tears. That is the picture I saw that night on the shores of the Pacific, listening to Thomas and God. It was as if his tears were falling directly onto the feet of Jesus. I'm not saying that every single time we speak to God, in a thought or a Good Morning or a prayer of thanks that it is imperative we end up prostrate on the ground in sobs.

But I long to pray that way—intimately. And He longs to feel our broken tears.

Boom

If I could do it all again (not life, just working at the Children's Home) I would have more picnics. I would spend more time out in the insect-infested field, guzzling sweet tea and enjoying the presence of my girls, during the very few moments when all the social barriers and popularity stigmas are cast aside and all who are present are momentarily allowed to genuinely enjoy each other's presence. The picnic attendees were always stoked at first, eager to eat, eager to chat, eager for the picnic tradition. But sooner or later, the crowd would dwindle. One by one, they would retreat indoors to wait for a phone call or start on homework or watch their favorite sitcom.

And although I was always sad to see these very rare everyone's-getting-along occasions end, I looked forward to it at the same time. It seems that candor and vulnerability rarely show up in large numbers. And it seemed that it was when there were only a select few, or one young woman remaining on our rank picnic blanket that I was really allowed to see through the sky-high steel walls built up through years of rejection, abuse, and disappointment, and gaze straight into their souls.

The first time I ever saw the real Sara was during one such picnic. All other picnic attendees had wandered back indoors, and there we sat, in the still splendor of the setting sun. I don't remember how the conversation began or even how it ended. But I remember somewhere in the middle screaming out to God with all the silent strength I could muster, begging Him to break her—to let me in.

Sara talked about her family, or lack thereof. She talked about her brother Kody and her mother Karen (whom she referred to only as 'Karen' and never as 'Mom') and her foster-family back home in Alabama with whom she had lived for two years. She talked about the other girls in our house and how as messed up as their specific situations and families were—at least they had someone to claim them. At least they had someone to call their own.

She did her first line of crack at 16, while sitting at the kitchen table with her mother and her mother's boyfriend. Her biological father left the scene when she was three months old, and she's seen him one time since then. The only male role models she knew growing up were the countless men in and out of her mother's life, some of which overlapped each other, resulting in quite a mess of a situation when two men woke to each other in bed, both waiting for Sara's mother to return home. The only other male figure in her life was her brother Kody, who was verbally and emotionally abusive throughout their childhood. The last update from Sara concerning Kody was that he called her a 'whore' for trading her body for shelter and a bed to sleep on. He told her she should be careful not to get caught, or the state would put her in the loony bin. Great guy.

Sara has moved 21 times and is not yet 18 years old. She has been to nine different public high schools. She has had first-hand experience with sex, drugs, alcohol, and abuse from a young age. And as I write, she is in hiding in an abandoned farmhouse, dependent entirely on the graciousness of others for food and clothing.

I don't remember what words of wisdom I had or didn't have to offer Sara that evening. But I remember clear as day what real Sara looked like, tears streaming down her softly freckled face, as she hurriedly wiped them away, knowing what a phenomenal risk she was taking in that moment by allowing just one more person who could potentially damage her to see her pain. You may think it is nothing out of the ordinary for a hormonal teenage girl to weep as she poured out her heart under the red-orange summer sky. But this girl, no matter how hormonal or attention-seeking at times she could be—she didn't cry, *ever*. And as much as I wanted her to continue to break before me just as I had asked, to please just let me in, at the same time I wanted to grab her by the shoulders and shake her out of it. I wanted to tell her,

"Sara!!! Be careful. Please be careful who you let in. Be cautious even of me. I have the potential to wound you as well, you know. I may one day leave you as well."

And I did.

I did leave her as well. And now I sit in my guest house in Entebbe, Uganda, East Africa, drowning out the dozens of mosquitoes with Sister Hazel blasting through my sound-proof headphones—I wonder as I write. I wonder if she is warm enough tonight, with her seven blankets to keep out the wintry night air. I wonder who brought her food today, or if she ate at all. I wonder if she's gained any of the 25 lbs back that she's lost since the day she decided she wasn't beautiful, because no one had ever convinced her otherwise. I wonder if she's scared staying in an abandoned farmhouse out in the country all alone as a 17 year old fugitive. I wonder if she really plans on living in hiding until her 21st birthday, when the State of Missouri will no longer maintain custody. I wonder if I'm just like Kody or Karen or the Camericks or her sleazy, cheating high school boyfriend—just one more person who left her.

Just one more lost hope.

———— ((◦)) ————

Back in the days of the Roman empire, adoption looked quite a bit different than it does these days. These days, a young girl can be 'adopted' into a family even to the point of taking on a new last name, and then be given back to be a ward of the state upon learning "she is just too hard to handle." Back then the adopted were not chosen at random and placed in foster-to-adopt family placements, which were all but permanent, making the term 'adoption' not necessarily exciting to the child involved, as it may or may not actually go through. During the first century, an adoption meant that the son to be adopted was *chosen*. He was specifically hand-picked by the father, and inferior in no way to the other sons. Adoption meant that the entire history of specified son was completely erased, including past family, past wrongs, past and past identity. With a new name came not just a new family, but a new identity. The adoption could never be reversed. Unlike the adoption processes of current-day America, a family could not simply give up or give back an adopted son. A biological son could be disowned, but an adopted son was *permanent*. The adoption could never be reversed. It was complete.

This is why our adoption into the family of God is so beautiful; because not only were we intentionally chosen, but the adoption is eternal. We will never be given up. Perhaps this is why God created us, in essence knowing that we would fall to sin. Because He knew that we would one day be sons of Him, rather than of Adam. He knew the adoption would take place, and He would rather us be sons of Him, than of Sin.

I want Sara to know she's been adopted. I want her to know she's been deliberately chosen, and not rejected. I want her to know the adoption she is under is permanent. It can't be annulled. She can't be given up. She can't be deceived. She can't be packed and carted across the states like some sort of commodity. I want her to know this adoption I speak of isn't through the State of Missouri, or Alabama or any other state. I want her to know she is the daughter of the most all-powerful, all-loving, ever-constant unconditional King in all the world and universe and beyond. I want her to know she can never really and truly have *no one* ever again.

And my hope is that you and I may come to know the same.[13]

---

[13] This journal entry/story was written during my first month's stay in Entebbe, Uganda. I learned within that month that Sara had run from the Chilrden's Home the day I flew out to Africa. She effectively remained in hiding for three months until she was released from DHS custody after her 18th birthday. Sara is now married with two children and living with her husband in southwest Missouri. I was able to be at the hospital on the day of her first child's birth, as promised. I keep in touch with and see her regularly.

Notes from America:

ON LOVING OTHERS

*A Short Story

Once upon a world, there existed a beautiful country called *Timor*[14]. This nation was full of the types of people who strongly believed they had a right to own certain things and practice certain freedoms. And there came a time when a neighboring country decided to expand their borders and take these freedoms away from Timor.

Timor feared they may soon come under a sort of tyrannical rule, and in fearing the worst, decided to call upon their powerful ally *Virtus*[15] to come across the deep blue and fight for them to ensure their freedom was secure. Virtus, being a sort of world power, readily agreed to fight for such a cause, knowing how violated they would feel if they were the ones about to lose their freedoms. The people of Virtus thought of the horrors of a tyrannical rule. They envisioned a ghastly place of dwelling where all lived equally and communally. They dreamt of sharing all they owned and working together for shared money

---

14   Latin meaning= *fear*
15   Latin meaning= *virtue*

that would be evenly distributed so not a mouth would be left unfilled. The thought of such a place, such a sour existence where control and right to individual power and wealth were nonexistent, boiled their blood and soured their dreams.

And so, the nation of Virtus set out to remedy the problem at hand. They would go to fight for the weaker country, Timor. They would go to Timor and set them free. And they would do it in the simplest, quickest way. They would extinguish the threat. The enemy, the nation called *Avaritia*[16], would be slowly moving in on Timor, and Virtus would be there to greet them with open arms. Because the people of Virtus held such a great sense of pride for themselves and their nation, they worried they may lose too great a number of lives in sending their own across the sea to fight for Timor. And so, they made sure to take every possible precaution in sending their army away. They were trained with the utmost care and precision, and each man or woman sent to fight went across the sea knowing and believing the more fathers and sons and brothers and husbands they shot in the head or chest or threw a grenade upon, the more likely Timor was to see their freedom secured.

The armies of Virtus fought well and killed many; but many of their own were lost as well. A great number of those sent away to secure Timor's freedom returned home to Virtus, and upon arriving back safely were neither thanked nor recognized for the sacrifice they made abroad. Meanwhile, the great nation of Virtus was in the middle of yet another crisis.

Too many people were becoming pregnant unintentionally, and

---

16   Latin meaning= *greed*

Virtus feared overpopulation was soon to come. This obviously threatened the comfortable lifestyle in which they lived. In order to take care of such unfortunate situations as pregnancies due to rape, broken condoms, and drunken 'mistakes,' Virtus thought it best to dispose of this unwanted populous. Because they wanted to get as much use as possible out of the unwanted, they decided to let the pregnant women carry to term, and then send the unwanted children across the sea to Avaritia, as a sort of payment or peace offering to the nation, which happened to be lacking in children of the superior nation.

Avaritia welcomed the Virtus children gladly and soon after greeting them stacked them on the battlefields in piles with their own unwanted and shot them to pieces. This was their way of expressing thanks to Virtus for the offering they had made.

Upon hearing of the great slaughter taking place in Avaritia, Virtus became outraged and decided they must act quickly to stop such an abhorrent thing. After much debate and thought-provoking discussion involving the politicians as well as religious leaders of the time, they finally agreed upon a solution.

They would recruit new troops and send them out to replace those Virtus innocents who had been slaughtered and entirely immobilize the former plan of action. To the leaders of Virtus, most especially those who were considered religious and politically conservative, it seemed to make much more sense to sacrifice grown men and women who already had families, careers, and lifetime relationships than to sacrifice those innocent souls who had none of the above.

And so, the troops were sent, the war was fought, and the nation of Virtus successfully destroyed a few million lives, only losing around 60,000 themselves. Fortunately, hundreds of thousands of young innocents' lives were saved when replaced by troops, and they were able to grow up in various group homes, detention centers, lock-down facilities, and foster homes, only after spending the first formative years of their lives in the sexually abusive homes of their biological families.

Virtus continued to grow as a nation of pride and superiority, making sure to carefully calculate which lives were of more value than others when the problem of war and tyranny again presented itself. The nation survived and thrived for the most part, only encountering minor problems such as trillion-dollar deficits here and there and perhaps a minor oil spill disaster now and again. Thankfully, Virtus had such great rapport with the rest of the world, the nations came in droves to help with such disasters, knowing if the time came when their political freedom were on the line, Virtus would be ready and willing to kill millions for the cause.

Homeless Gary

After I graduated from college I spent the summer in New Orleans as one of six interns at a summer camp called MissionLab. The camp was focused entirely on active missions—*doing* rather than simply *hearing*.

Whereas the majority of summer church camps offer mostly entertainment, teaching, games, more entertainment, more games, and a little more teaching—MissionLab was geared entirely around serving, and because this was shortly after the devastation of Hurricane Katrina had hit New Orleans, there was definitely not a shortage of service project opportunities.

The usual camper schedule consisted of daily morning video devotions in the Price building led by our video-tech/brother-to-the-boss/inspirational preacher, while myself and fellow interns lounged on bean-bag chairs in the back, keeping our eyes on things while inhaling ridiculous amounts of Starbucks coffee, as we had risen at 5:30a.m. that morning and gone to bed at 2:30a.m. the night before. As soon as devotions were over the campers headed to the café for some southern-style grub. I personally ate heavily buttered grits every single morning, solely to prove I was not the city-slicker 'yank' my entire staff seemed to think I was. And then, it was off to various project sites for the day.

Not all of our project-sites were about gutting or yard work or hard labor. Some churches were assigned to work at inner-city daycares, or organizing thrift stores and food pantries. And still some were to go to the French Quarter to hand out sandwiches and Jesus to the homeless of New Orleans. There was also the work in the wetlands which consisted of planting various foliage such as bulrush in the bayous in order to rehabilitate the plant-life of the city. These types of projects were led by the hemp-loving, no-bra wearing, green-thumb type.

The most impactful moment I experienced that summer amidst the ruins of a great American city did not occur 'on-site.' It was not while sweating liters of orange Gatorade in a full-body tyvex suit and face mask, while bashing espestus-walls with a sledgehammer. It was not while performing impromptu puppet shows for the quite inattentive toddlers at daycare, or while having a country-music sing-a-long with Raymond Road Baptist in our 15-passenger van while getting lost in the city for the 5th time in 2 days. It was not during one of many heart-to-hearts I had with hurting high school girls. Nor was it seeing Betty, who had lived in a 45x5ft. FEMA trailer in her front yard since the hurricane, walk into her home and for the first time in over two years see walls in her kitchen.

As touching and memorable as all afore-mentioned experiences were—as real as God was to me in all of these moments, there is still another that stands above them all.

The moment I believe I truly saw my Savior's face, was not at any particular project-site with any particular church; it was not during a phenomenal sermon on Love or the last worship service of the summer. It was on the streets of the French Quarter, with a man named Gary.

MissionLab was over for the summer, and in celebration of its finale, the entire staff went to the Quarter for a night on the town. We all dressed up for the occasion (and by that I mean we did not wear torn and painted jeans and mud-stained T-shirts) and went to quite the classy Seafood Restaurant. So classy, in fact, that the napkins were cloth rather than paper and the water was served in stemmed glasses.

Summer interns don't make much money.

So although we did eat well all summer, aside from the turkey or ham on stale white bread sandwiches we had for lunch every single day, we hadn't eaten *this* well all summer. It was quite a big deal, really. Even the camp directors joined in for the evening. Being that we were at a Seafood Restaurant and I am not a fan at all of seafood—I hate it, in fact. I was a bit concerned that I would not find anything too tantalizing on the menu.

But oh, how wrong I was.

I found, on the menu, a meal consisting of a honey-bourbon marinated, grilled salmon, asparagus, and garlic mashed potatoes. Basically, all 3 of my very favorite foods in the entire world were on one plate. The perfect meal. I must confess, I was confused as to why salmon was being served in a Seafood Restaurant, when clearly, salmon was lakefood (any fish that is found in freshwater) and not seafood. But my entire staff proceeded to argue that salmon was, in fact seafood, and in the end we agreed to disagree. It only mattered that this most-amazing of restaurants was about to serve me the best meal I would ever partake of in this life.

Then came the appetizers. Fried pickles dipped generously in ranch dressing quickly became my new favorite delicacy. Fried and grilled alligator was also thoroughly enjoyed. The more I ate the more I began to salivate over my soon-to-be served heaven-on-a-plate. I antsy, irritated, and frequented the ladies' room as I continuously inhaled my chilled water in anxious anticipation.

And then it happened.

My lakefood came.

I could hardly believe my hungry eyes—which stayed open and staring down at my plate all throughout the everlasting prayer of thanks. The second the 'amen' was said I dove into my salmon—and asparagus—and garlic mashed potatoes. The best I had ever eaten, or ever would eat. And just about 3.2 minutes into this glorious, much-anticipated meal, it hit me.

I was full.

"Full!?!?" I thought.

May it never be.

And so I continued to eat, a few small and very forced bites and stopped when I felt I might actually regurgitate fried pickles and gator at any given moment. I sat, glumly, staring down at my nearly full plate, devastated. For another hour or so, we sat, while the rest of the still-hungry crew devoured their meals. I continued to enjoy the surrounding company, but was inwardly appalled that I was unable to partake of my long-awaited best meal of all time. I got my hands on a take-away box as soon as possible so at least I wouldn't have to continue drooling over the food I could not eat.

What seemed like hours later, the rest of the crew finished their meals, the bill was paid and we all rolled out of the restaurant towards our next destination—Café du Monde[17]

It was while we walked the streets of the Quarter towards Café du Monde that I first spotted Gary.

He was homeless.

I'm not sure how exactly one can know someone is homeless, except that you just sort of know. The clothes are stained

---

17   For those of you who have been to the New Orleans Café du Monde—I need not expound upon its greatness, you already know. For those of you whom have not ever visited Café due Monde, allow me to expound upon its greatness. The French Quarter is called the French Quarter b/c it was settled and inhabited by the French. Café du Monde, is a French coffee and beignet shop which amazingly, is open 24 hours a day, seven days a week. Beignets are basically exactly like a funnel cake, except shaped like a small triangle rather than a funnel, and with 3x as much powdered sugar heaped on top. Served along with these oh-so-healthy beignets, is coffee, or café a lait, which is ½ coffee, ½ milk. So pretty much, the best coffee and dessert combo anyone could ever hope for.

and torn, the hair matted. There is usually a certain 'home-less stench' that accompanies a homeless person. And lastly but probably most obvious is the homeless stride. The sagging shoulders, lowered head, hopeless swagger that seems to scream *HOMELESS* loud and clear. And such was Gary. Less than 20 yards from Café du Monde, hunched over on a park bench directly under the fluorescent city lights, across from the historic canon that faces St. Louis Cathedral, sat homeless Gary.

It took less than a millisecond altogether for me to make eye contact with, recognize as homeless, and of course, perform the oh-so-familiar, jerking of the head, instant cessation of eye contact, quick analyzation of how it must be his own fault he was homeless and I can do nothing to help, change of subject of thought, and brisk walk away from uncomfortable moment at hand. And so I continued, with my box of heavenly salmon and garlic and mashed potatoes and asparagus in hand, past Homeless Gary and on towards Calorie Kingdom. Allow me to reiterate. . .

And so I continued *past Homeless Gary…*

And then a record-breaking quick conversation with God:

"AmyRose," God said.
"Crap," I responded.

I scanned my surroundings and decided upon intern Stacy Ellis. She seemed to love all people fairly naturally and also happened to be twice my stature and strength so she was really a perfect pick for fellow evangelist/bodyguard. Box of $30 gourmet leftovers in hand, Stacy and I made our way back to the bench where Homeless Gary sat. I really had not a clue as to what I was going to say to Homeless Gary. What exactly is the best subject of conversation when approaching the homeless?

So, where are you from?

(Blank Stare)

Where do you work?

"I don't."

Where do you stay?

"Depends on the weather. If it's raining, under the overpass. If not, this bench will do."

So I tried to start as simply as possible-asking an obvious question to which I already knew the answer.

Hello sir. Would you like some food?

I try to refer to all men as 'sir', but I especially like to call homeless men 'sir' because I don't think they would ever in a million years think themselves worthy of the term; and that's what makes it beautiful.

Of course Homeless Gary wanted some food.

As he reached for the box I proceeded to ask if it would be all right for the two of us to have a seat with him while he enjoyed the delicious salmon that I suddenly became hungry for all over again now that it was in someone else's hands. Stacy and I seated ourselves on either side of him, barely fitting on the bench. As he devoured my leftovers I quickly began calculating how exactly I would go about converting Homeless Gary within the next few minutes, before he finished his free meal and no longer had a good reason to sit with two perfect strangers. But as usual, God's plan was a bit different than mine, and as He began to guide my speech I soon realized this conversation was probably not leading to the 'Sinner's Prayer.' Homeless Gary and I talked about the places he had lived—not the places as in the various overpasses or cardboard box shacks or park benches; I mean places like various cities. We talked about his family or lack thereof. We talked about how he liked living in New Orleans. And as we made small-talk, with every word he breathed into my conservative Christian lungs the sinful scent of cheap whisky.

Does it ever get cold at night here? I asked.

"Probably. But I don't notice. That's why I drink. When you're full of whisky, you see, you don't feel the cold. Or the wind. Or the rain. You're just numb—so you're ok."

That was the point at which I actually felt my heart break inside of my sober, neatly clothed, expensive-perfume-scented chest.

"You're just numb—so you're ok."

I don't know that I have ever heard such empty words. And I don't know that I have ever in my life seen such eyes. When Homeless Gary's eyes met mine it was as if I were actually looking into the face of God. His were the deepest, bluest, most intoxicating eyes I have ever seen. A little glazed over. Tired. Hopeless.

But mostly, *broken.*

Before Stacy and I headed back to the crew at Café du Monde, I asked Homeless Gary if it would be all right if we prayed with him. I grabbed his cool leathery hands in mine and the four of us met together for a moment. Stacie, Homeless Gary, God and I. I don't remember what I prayed. No idea. I know it wasn't long or glorious or ultra-spiritual. But I know it was divine. Because it was a divine appointment that had brought me to Homeless Gary that night. From living in my Baptist bubble within SBU, to my Baptist bubble at the seminary, to the streets of the most disgusting, and wretched of places in all of the U.S., to that Seafood Restaurant Where I longed for the ultimate heaven-on-a-plate that I could not even enjoy, back to the streets of New Orleans to Homeless Gary.

You may be wondering why I refer to him as 'Homeless Gary' rather than simply Gary. There is a reason. The reason is that 'Homeless Gary' is much more uncomfortable than simply "Gary." Homeless Gary reminds me, every time I pen the words, *Homeless Gary* that I met face-to-face with Jesus. I met face-to-face with Homeless Jesus.

Hungry.
Hopeless.
Broken.

Homeless Gary was "the least of these" and I had almost passed him by.

Not almost. I did pass him by.

If you remember, I didn't stop to feed Homeless Gary, I *came back* to feed him. And that is due solely to the fact that he was *Homeless* Gary and not just *Gary*. Feeding my co-workers or a sister or an adorable and well-kept 8 year old who happened to be standing in the streets with a family nearby and happened to love salmon and asparagus and garlic mashed potatoes—any of these people—any of these normal and usual and whole people would have been easy to feed.

But not Homeless Gary. He was not so easy to feed. He was not so easy to look at. He reeked of cheap whisky. His hair was matted. His jeans and shirt stained. His shoes worn. But mostly, his eyes broken. He looked homeless. And so it was uncomfortable.

And so I passed him by.

Because, like Homeless Gary—I much preferred to remain numb.

I Love Abortion

On my way to the Fayetteville public library this afternoon, I was stopped at a red light on College Avenue and noticed a young girl holding a cardboard sign that read "free hangers!" She had several hangers on the arm of the hand holding the sign, and a cigarette in her other hand.

I became overly excited upon realizing the possibility of free hangers, and thoroughly contemplated pulling over to take her up on this amazing offer. *Isn't Arkansas just fantastic!?* I thought to myself. *Free hangers! I've never seen such a thing. Someone is seriously standing on the street corner offering free hangers, just because she can. Just because who doesn't always need another hanger or two?*

The light changed to green and my day-dreaming ceased. I hit the gas and took one last glance at Hanger-girl. . .and realized she was not alone. About 30 yards away from Hanger-girl was Mohawk-boy, who also happened to be holding a sign. Only his sign did not read "Free Hangers!" rather,

I LOVE ABORTION!

I was horrified.

Hanger-girl was not, in fact, standing on the street corner sim-ply to offer an arm-full or so of free hangers to anyone in need. Hanger-girl was holding an arm-full of hangers because she was trying to prove a point, and she was using some sort of sick joke to do so. Hangers, get it? Back in the day when abortion was ille-gal, abortion 'doctors' would stick hangers up a woman and just slice the "fetus" right up. In fact, apparently this is still practiced today by less-fortunate women who cannot afford an abortion. So, in order to promote women's rights, here's a hanger and a hilarious sign about cutting babies up with hangers!

I kept driving.

I drove to the library and attempted to forget about the scene I had just witnessed, as I printed off a forbearance form for my student loans and browsed the library's c.d. collection to see if there was anything worth renting. But I did not forget what I had seen. Not even for a second. And so as I pulled out of the library parking lot, I decided I would go the long way home and stop and have a chat with Hanger-girl.

I parked on the street corner at a real-estate building, and upon exiting my car was viciously glared at by the woman behind the glass who pounded on the window and pointed at me to move my car before she had it towed. I then made my way down the sidewalk and towards Hanger-girl, thinking out loud, "God. WHAT am I doing, exactly?"

I started the conversation by explaining how thrilled I was about free hangers—and how disappointed I was upon realizing they were not, in fact, free or available to whoever was in need. She felt bad for me, I think, and asked if I wanted one. "Yes, I do, actually."

I made small-talk, hanger in hand, and asked if she was there with an organization or just on her own. I asked if she was cold, and she said yes. So I asked her if she would like a coffee, half-expecting her to completely reject my offer. She accepted, and in a matter of minutes I was back in my car and on my way to a coffee shop to purchase two cappuccinos with the last remaining $6 I had to my name.

Two cappuccinos later, I was back in my car and driving towards the scene, contemplating whether or not it was worth it to park in the same parking lot I had earlier and risk getting my car towed. And as I drove, I noticed something I had not seen before. Across the street from Hanger-girl and Mo-hawk boy, were Pro-Life activists, all of whom were holding signs that read such things as "Thank your Mom for choosing Life!", "Abortion Kills Babies!" etc.

And so, feeling rather radical, I immediately pulled over and parked in front of the walk-in abortion clinic. Let me just say, I was the pastor's kid who grew up on the OTHER side of the road, holding up the "Abortion Kills" signs. We were the family that stayed out from dawn til' dusk promoting 'life' with all the other good Christians.

Yet here I was, 15 or so years later, parked proudly in front of a walk-in clinic, bringing cappuccinos to the 'enemy.' I smiled widely as I walked, a cappuccino in each hand, and voiced my thoughts to God.

"God. I feel like I am being born again. . . again."

I delivered my cappuccinos with a massive smile and then stood next to Hanger-girl attempting yet again to make small-talk, while my former teammates stood across the road with signs in hand, glaring at my very presence, probably wondering how I had been so quickly recruited to 'the dark side.'

Hanger-girl: Thanks for the coffee!

Me: Oh, you're welcome! I'm glad I found a coffee shop. I just moved here and usually get lost every time I attempt to go anywhere.

Hanger-girl: We were sort of wondering if maybe you put laxatives in this or something. You know, maybe tried to poison us.

Me: (awkwardly laughing) Haha . . .no, not this time. That's a good idea though! So, have more people given you hate glares or been supportive and honked?

Hanger-girl: Honestly? We have had very few people yell at us—only a couple actually. Most honk and wave and are supportive. Someone did call the cops on us, but the cops basically just told us to make sure to stay on the sidewalk and out of the street and it was fine.

At this point I am nervously contemplating how exactly I'm going to fit Jesus into the conversation. You know, give her the

4-1-1 of how abortion is in fact, murder, but Jesus loves her and so do I. Because, why else would I go to all this trouble if I wasn't going to leave having won a soul to Christ?

Me: Can I ask you something?

Hanger-girl: Yeah, sure.

Me: Do you get easily offended?

Hanger-girl: Not really. Unless I see someone like— murdering a cat or something.

Me: (again, nervous chuckle) Haha. Well, I mean, would you be offended if I asked you something about abortion?

Hanger-girl: Uh, maybe

Me: (on second thought, maybe now is not the time to attempt to win a soul) Oh. Well, I just want to say that I'm actually very pro-life. But I think that what you and your friend are doing out here is quite ballsy, and I personally don't think I'd ever have the guts to do such a thing. I think it's neat that you are willing to stand up for something you believe in, and I admire that in you.

I wanted to ask her if there was anything she needed prayer for. I wanted to climb up on a giant soap box right there on College Avenue and tell her that I used to be in the crowd across the street. I wanted to tell her that I grew up holding the pro-life signs and standing for hours and walking for miles thinking I was saving lives. I wanted to tell her that "I'm not one of *those* Christians" anymore. I wanted to tell her a lot of things.

But it happened to be rush-hour and we happened to be on the busiest street in town. And in between the honks and yells and whistles and cars this meaningful conversation wasn't exactly happening. Ultimately, Hanger-girl was distracted, and not entirely interested in what I had to say. Perhaps it was the "I'm pro-life, by the way" that threw her off.

I told Hanger-girl it was very nice meeting her and Hector (young man with I LOVE ABORTION sign) and I hoped they stayed warm. I walked to my car, still defiantly parked in front of the abortion clinic, and pulled out onto College Ave. When I pulled up to the light, Hector was standing there, sign in hand, looking right at me. I waved over-excitedly and with the grandest smile I've had in a while, still overwhelmed with the whole ordeal. And Hector smiled back, and waved valiantly, and then threw a "rock on" hand in the air with his free hand.

As I drove away I couldn't help but feel I had somehow failed. I'm not exactly sure what my intention was. I suppose I wanted to love them. And I suppose that's what I did. But naturally, growing up on the pro-life side of College Avenue, I wanted to convert them. I wanted to give them cappuccino and Jesus, not just cappuccino.

I wanted to change their minds.

But standing on the 'wrong' side of the road got me to wondering. I wonder if we as Christians are standing on the 'right' side of the road after all. What exactly were we accomplishing all those hours—all those years that we "walked for life"? If holding up "Abortion Kills" signs outside of clinics where hopeless teenage girls and single mothers and rape victims is meant to stir emotion and cause guilt, then yes, we have absolutely accomplished something. But is that really an accomplishment to be proud of?

Maybe we should reconsider which side of the road we stand on.

I'm pretty sure if Jesus walked the earth in flesh today, He would not be holding "Abortion is MURDER" signs outside a clinic solely to invoke guilt. From what I know of Him, He would be more focused on loving the Hanger-girl across the street.

An Apology (unexcused)

I was at a meeting once—a sort of church 'community group' in which we ate, sang, prayed and talked about God and things of life. Our group consisted of mostly U of A[18] students, a few graduates, one St. Louis native, and a very wise, white-bearded man name Mike.

Bobby and Judy were the hosts of the group, our "fearless leaders" as we called them. But it was assumed that every week, no matter who led the discussion and what the specified topic was, at some point throughout the evening Mike would insert a few words of wisdom or ask some sort of deep and thought-provoking question.

Our group was one full of mostly extroverted people, none of whom feared having the floor or speaking their mind. And at times, there was almost a fight for it. One particular evening, a friend was making a comment, the discussion became lively, and Mike sort of—stole the spotlight. I don't think anyone noticed.

It was subtle and what he had to say was, as usual, wise and good. But nonetheless, someone else was in the middle of a thought and he stole the lead. The discussion continued. Not one of us blinked and I'm pretty sure no one even noticed what happened.

But Mike did. And he made a point to speak out as soon as a moment of silence hit the air.

"Justin," he said, "I'm sorry. I cut you off and I shouldn't have. I didn't mean to rebut what you were saying and I should have let you finish your thought. I'm sorry."

And what did Mike's words of wisdom consist of only five minutes previous to the scene I just described? Confession.

Mike challenged us to confess *without excuse*. He brought to light the fact that nine times out of ten, when we confess, when we apologize for an action or a comment or a decision, we immediately follow the confession with a reason we did it.

We follow it with an excuse.

> "I'm sorry I raised my voice at you, but I was angry."
> "I'm sorry I assumed the worst of you and the situation, but I was just going by what you usually do."
>
> "I'm sorry I stood you up, but I got sidetracked."
>
> "I'm sorry I interrupted, but I had to make my point before I forgot."
>
> "I'm sorry my race/religion tried to kill off yours, but we were just trying to protect ourselves and our freedom. And besides, that's in the past."

Here is a prime example of why we love Mike. Because he walks the walk. Mike gave us this morsel of Truth about how our confessions are limited to excuse, and when he made a mistake, he stopped the discussion, brought to light when he felt he had wronged a friend, made an apology, and left it at that.

"I just finished telling you that we need to confess without excuse, and that's exactly what I need to do right now. Justin, I'm sorry. I shouldn't have done that."

I'm sorry. I was wrong. End of story.

I wonder what the world would look like—what relationships would look like—if confessions were left at that. Void of excuse.

And I am beginning to wonder what my own confession would look like without excuse. . .

I am selfish. More often than not, I think of myself first. I am often late to work, regardless of how it affects my clients and my co-workers. I would rather spend my money on myself and my own needs and wants than on the wants and needs of others. I would rather buy a new outfit or go out to eat than budget $30 a month to feed a starving child half a world away. If there is food on the table that needs to feed a group I will make sure to get a plate first. I eat the last donut and use the last cereal bowl of milk. I am quick to stereotype and quick to judge. I naturally despise those who have more money, or are more privileged than myself.

And for all of the above and much more, *I am sorry.*

*Once Upon a Mountain

Once upon a time, there was a man named Brad. Brad stood about 6'2" with thick, black hair and chocolate eyes. His complexion was dark and his skin rough from living rather than observing. Brad lived in Oregon at the foot of the Cascades and was what some may call a 'revolutionary.' He was a man set apart, and often isolated from others by choice rather than bad luck or happenstance.

He heard from God frequently and made sure that others knew it. Brad was strong and solid and sure. When he spoke it seemed as though God Himself was in the room, and had supernaturally borrowed Brad's body, consuming his flesh and moving Brad's mouth to His voice like some sort of life-size Pinocchio.

God would speak words of wisdom and revelation through Brad frequently and often times the Truth spoken was neither comforting nor welcomed by the hearers. When Brad spoke he called people out on their complacent, stagnant lives. He challenged them to recognize that idolatry today is not kissing a golden god but, rather, staring into the face of comfort and complacency and welcoming their deathly grasp. Brad told people who God is. And if they didn't like Him then tough luck, He's God, He's in charge, and if you tick Him off or disobey then there's hell to pay . . .literally.

Then one day Brad made the wrong person angry. He said the 'wrong' thing to a girl he just so happened to be interested in and he became so terrified of the possible repercussions that he ran away. Brad ran away to the mountains. He packed his Kelty pack, laced up his boots, jumped into his Outback and fled for fear of his very life. Perhaps he did not fear his life. But in the moment when her fiery eyes met his and the ice-cold stare was delivered he truly believed his life was on the line.

And so—he ran to the mountains. He parked his car at the foot of Mt. Hood and began the ascent to safety. Although his 6'2" frame was full of heart and muscle, he found himself becoming winded as he trekked. Perhaps because his wandering was more of an anxious run—a fearful escape from the piercing eyes which he fled.

Brad crossed ravines and moss beds and miniature falls. He scurried through pines and did not stop to smell the blue mountain air or watch the fox scamper from his hole. In time, his fearful sprint became a jog, then a walk, then a swagger. Brad happened upon a cave and, exhausted, crawled inside, crouching against the sweaty wall and hugging his knees. As he sat he pondered . . . As he pondered he wondered . . . he wondered he questioned. He questioned God. Brad wanted to know if God cared. If He cared that he was doing just as he was told. Declaring the brutal Truth. If He cared that he was being ultimately rejected. If He cared that Brad was alone.

So he began to whisper to God.

Speak. Please speak!

Brad wanted to hear from God. And because God seemed to be in the heavens, Brad logically assumed the best way to hear from Him would be to get as near to the heavens as he physically could. Mt. Hood bragged a 14,000 –foot peak, and Brad had decided in the morning he would reach the summit.

———=》《(◦)》《=———

Brad awoke to the warm Oregon sun beating down on his face and shoulder. He choked down some stale jerky, guzzled a quart of water, and began his journey to the voice of God.

Thin air—sparse.
Panting . . .heaving.
Racing.
Grieving.
Slowly
    Slowly
        Slowly
Climbing.
A struggle
A fight.
Through shadows of trees.

Rocks
And crevices
Sweat
And
pain.
And soon enough
Traveler sees his gain . . .

THE SUMMIT!

Brad collapsed. He embraced the earth beneath him, kissing it as he lay prostrate on this holy ground. He kissed it until his mouth was full of dirt and gristle and when he felt the earth mix with his saliva he did not spit it out in disgust, but treasured the reality of the victory at hand. Brad simply lay, soaking up the beauty of his surroundings in the ecstasy of the moment—the summit he had reached. He continued to lay. In silence and empty thought. And then—in awestruck wonder. He had reached the summit and knew that soon he would be witnessing the mighty Hand of God. Heaving himself from his prostrate position on to his shaky knees, he turned to face the blazing sun, lifting his arms towards the heavens,

Speak!

Brad cried out. He did not ask that God speak. He did not hope. He did not yell or even scream his request . . .he cried. And a true cry comes only from the deepest, most intimate depths of an utterly broken soul.

Silence.

Seconds passed. Then minutes. Then hours. Still, silence.

And then, a mighty wind. It was not a wind that started slowly and swelled into something great; it was sudden and glory and power. In an instant, Brad was thrown to the hard ground, the breath taken right from his lungs for just a moment. The wind was so powerful it cleared the ground beneath him. The surrounding cliffs were shattered like glass shards and strewn about him. It lasted several seconds and Brad was sure he would soon hear God's voice—he was sure His very presence was in this mighty wind.

Silence. God was not in the wind.

"SPEAK!" Brad cried out.

And seconds, then moments, then hours passed. Still, silence. Brad began to doze, while kneeling on the empty land. And suddenly the earth beneath him began to quiver—and then to rumble—and then to violently shake. The very ground on which he knelt split beneath him, and he desperately scrambled to find a solid place. Although enveloped with fear, his doubting heart was now hopeful as well—hopeful this most deadly of silence was soon to be broken.

But the earth shook and the mount crumbled, and still, God did not speak. Brad's hope transformed to anger. He had been at the summit since sunrise and still God had not spoken. What could be the meaning of His silence? Had God chosen to reject Brad even after all he had done for Him? He had sought after God—he had spoken for Him, sacrificed for Him, climbed for Him.

In anger Brad again cried out, "God—my God—speak! Father speak! Savior speak! I am here! I am here—please won't you speak!!!!"

Brad begged. He pleaded with all his broken soul, as tears streaked his dirt-stained, sun kissed face. And in time, Brad's anger turned to fierce rage. Kneeling, he pounded the bare ground until his fists stained the earth a crimson red. Brad's rage gave way to hopelessness. He lay in doubt—but mostly, in disappointment. Though up until now Brad had been slightly chilled by the elevation and cool mountain breeze, he found himself beginning to heavily perspire.

The ground below him began to burn the soles of his boots, his clothes now dripping, stuck to his frame. Brad leaped from the ground to the crag above him, tripping along the way. As he crouched atop his safety crag, he watched as steam began to rise from the earth below him. Brad's vision began to blur as his head spun.

Heat. Starving. Thirsty. On the verge of passing out and then—Fire.

Where once there was steam, columns of fire now rose and fell and thrashed about him. The flames never touched Brad. They surrounded him and taunted him and seemed to want to swallow him alive. But never did he feel their fiery sting.

"God," Brad said, "Finally—You are here." Patiently he watched the flames, wondering what magnificent thing God would have to say through such a demonstration of power.

The earth revived. The flames ceased. Where once the ground was split was no longer severed. The once misplaced rocks and leaves and earth were back in their place. The fallen trees now standing, the singed foliage, a spring green.

And God did not speak. It seemed to Brad that God had never been there at all. As if this whole experience was mere façade—hopeful imagination.

Brad closed his eyes and fell into a deep sleep.

He awoke mid-morning the following day. Brad laced his boots, swallowed the last of his water, and shouldered his pack. He closed his eyes, head back, face towards the heavens, arms hanging limp at his side. And then he turned, to make his way back down the mount. But Brad did not make it farther than a few weary steps. He thought he heard a voice—but was sure it was delirium—a simple hallucination due to lack of oxygen and dehydration. Brad stopped anyway. He dropped his pack to his feet and sat legs crossed, hands folded, gazing into the beauty of the mountain landscape displayed before him. Only this time, Brad did not cry out to God. He did not scream and plead and rant in disappointed rage. Brad sat in silence, and spoke not a word.

And then—God spoke. He chose to speak not in the wind, nor earthquake, nor fire. Instead, He came in a still, small voice—in fact, a whisper. A whisper so soft Brad nearly had to hold his breath to hear it.

"My child, you are not alone."

And Brad was very sure that he was not.

Thorncrown Independence

My first Arkansas Independence Day proved to be quite an eventful one. I was away from "home" and my traditional St. Louis arch fireworks experience, and as the Fourth drew closer I began debating whether or not I even supported the idea of what the holiday stood for anyway.

America's freedom.

Our religious rights and such were threatened so we responded in the obvious manner and killed just enough people to get those freedoms back.

Happy Independence Day.

As Arkansas is known for its natural beauty, especially recognizable in its abundance of rivers and trails, I decided to spend my independence weekend soaking up such natural beauty with a few co-worker friends while camping and canoeing the King's River.

The forecast for the weekend called for a 50% chance of rain and scattered storms, but our three-day weekend and outdoor itch convinced us it would be worth the risk. After getting lost for two and a half hours, making a total of twelve u-turns, and getting both of our pick-up trucks stuck four times in the mud, (at one point we had to recruit a nearby bulldozer-driver to pull us out) the five of us and Skippy, the black lab, boarded our ships and began our river adventure.

I was in a bit of a sore mood, as I did not entirely understand why we were just now commencing our river adventure three hours after leaving our campsite. But mostly I was having trouble wrapping my head around why exactly the men in our crew thought it was a good idea to start floating a river while heading directly into a thunderstorm. I love playing in the rain. What I do not love, is sitting in the rain, in a boat, on a river, for hours at a time. The trip turned out to be okay—okay in that we did not get struck by lightning or drown and we made it safely back to our only slightly soaked campsite just before nightfall (only after getting lost, yet again).

The following morning I regretfully woke up at approximately six o'clock and proceeded to drag Eric and Nicole out of their tent, convincing them that driving to town to locate a fresh cup of coffee was, in fact, quite a grand idea.

I had attempted to make my own 'cowboy coffee' the previous morning, failed utterly, and instead mooched a cup off the RV campers down the road. Both Eric and Nicole thought it was a great idea and were more than excited to go on my sunrise coffee hunt. I'm sure partially because there was a bit of unspoken tension between the crew back at the camp.

Eric played tour guide. We cruised through the great metropolis called Eureka Springs and he shared with us the beauty of historic homes, haunted hotels, downtown shops, and finally, off a back road nestled in the woods—the famous Thorncrown Chapel.

According to Eric, Thorncrown Chapel is some sort of fantastically beautiful place where the walls are made of glass and the place is booked for a year at a time because everyone wants to get married there. The three of us took a detour on our way back to camp and stopped by the place to check it out. There were several cars parked on the lot when we arrived and I wondered if there might be a service going on right then.

As we walked toward the path leading to the chapel we were stopped by a small-framed, curly-haired woman probably in her late fifties. She was holding bulletins, and as we approached the pathway where she stood between our destination and us she stopped us and inquired,

"Are you all here for the service?"

"No," Eric responded. "We just wanted to see the chapel; these girls have never seen it before."

"Oh. Well you'll have to come back then; we're having service now."

We didn't come back.

We climbed back into Eric's truck, packed up camp and went home. And as we drove, I realized something about myself I'm not sure I had previously recognized.

I realized I am angry.

As we walked away from the chapel that day my blood boiled. I immediately began ranting and raving to Eric and Nicole, questioning the reasoning behind the woman who turned us away.

"Is it because we were dressed in sweats, greasy-haired, and reeking of wood smoke? Did we not look like regular church-goers? Really? Is that what Jesus *really* would have done!?!? Turn people away? This is exactly why people hate Christians. What if I were someone that didn't grow up the way I did, in a Christian home? What if I knew nothing of Christ or Christianity at all, and what we just experienced was the only taste I ever got? Being turned away. Ridiculous."

They didn't seem to care quite as much about the incident as I did. Both were indifferent and even went as far as to defend the reasoning of the woman who turned us away, claiming "She probably just didn't want us to interrupt the service and be a distraction. . ."

But that was just my point. We were a distraction.

Since when are random passersby, tourists, campers, *people*—a "distraction" to a group of people claiming to be living examples of Jesus Christ—claiming to love as He loved? Unconditionally. Recklessly. Even when to do so is *inconvenient*.

A year earlier I don't think I would have been offended as I walked away from that chapel. Back then, I would have understood or at least empathized with the situation at hand, having been raised a pastor's daughter; I would have recognized what a frustrating 'distraction' a few campers could have caused. Back then, I could have walked away unharmed—untouched, even.

But that was back then. And back then I probably would have stood alongside the woman with the bulletins, nodding in agreement as she turned away the tourists. And back then the only place I'd ever lived was white, upper-middle-class suburbia, while attending white, private, college-preparatory schools, a Baptist university, and working under the Southern Baptist Convention for six years straight. And back then I believed what my parents believed because it made sense to, and I think mostly because I was scared not to.

But that was then. And this is now.

Now things are a bit different. These days I'm not required to sit through an hour and a half of Old Testament history twice a week in order to obtain a college degree. My co-workers don't believe things such as 'secular' music and alcohol are of the devil. I have lived in a place where being Caucasian I was by far the minority; and I can't say that every one of my nearest and dearest friends are "Christ-following," weekly churchgoers. In fact—only one of them falls into such a category. And not only am I okay with that, I am excited about it.

In Fayetteville, Arkansas the place to be on a Saturday night is Dickson Street. Lined with bars, hookah lounges, Sushi joints, venues and late-night coffee shops, it is every U of A college student's and young adult's place of choice. It is also the favorite hangout spot of fundie-evangelical Christians[19]. But the fundies don't come to have a beer or shoot some pool.

They come to protest.

They show up with ten-foot tall wooden crosses, standing on the corner of Dickson and West, praying for the sinners. They hold large poster boards proudly displaying such comforting phrases as,

Judgment comes first!

He who marries a divorced woman commits adultery.

And my personal favorite, *The woman is commanded to SUBMIT.*

I remember where I was the first time I saw the fundie[20] protestors. I was in a bar, sipping my poison, with a couple friends of mine. A bearded man came within two feet of our table, stared straight at me, and displayed his sign—

The drunkard is an abomination.

You can imagine my reaction. I was fuming. And Cade and

---

19   We shall call them "fundies."
20   The Term "fundie" refers to Christians who lay claim to conservative, fundamental beliefs and rely mostly on scriptural rules and regulations rather than embracing both Truth *and* Grace.

Jaymee got an earful. "One day," I loathed, "I'm going to come down here with my own sign! And I'm gonna' stand right next to them, or at least, realllly close to them! And *then* we'll see what happens!"

They were only slightly humored, but mostly disbelieving. Understandable, as most of the time when I have such grand ideas I don't actually follow through on them.

But this time I did.

I showed up on the corner of Dickson and West with my homemade sign during prime party time. As I did not want to appear to be making such a bold move purely out of spite, I first stopped to talk with the fundie-sign holders. Samuel and Joseph.

After talking with them for twenty minutes, I made my way to the street corner opposite them and began proudly displaying my rebuttal sign:

The Jesus I know of came to **LOVE**—*not to* condemn *and* judge. *And if he walked the streets today, he would be having a beer* with *you.*

Quite the social experiment, I must say. The fundies weren't really sure what to think of me. They simply stared straight ahead. And the other passersby? Responses varied greatly. Some assumed because I was holding a sign that I was there to condemn and angrily threw cigarettes and cuss-words at me, waving their arms in rage. Others whom actually stopped to read the sign offered high-fives, shouts of agreement, and some even offered a hug.

One quite intoxicated woman in her early thirties started screaming obscenities at me, flailing her arms—even lunging at me. She walked away still cursing and I followed her.

"You didn't even *read* it!" I yelled, while passionately waving my sign overhead.

So she did. She came back and read it. And then? Then she wept. So I held her. Right there on Dickson Street. I held her while she wept and repeatedly thanked me.

I still hear from her every now and then. She is attending AA meetings regularly and called once to tell me that I had "made an impression" on her. That I accepted her as is, no judgment cast, no questions asked. She said that I was "real" and that she wished there were more people in the world like me.

That phone call made it worth it. It made the awkwardness of standing on a street corner with a sign by myself, having cigarettes and obscenities and judgmental eyes thrown at me worth it.

———

And back to my original thought—realizing I am angry.

The outcome of my sign-holding was good. I touched some-one, and in the process, was touched and encouraged myself. I

was inspired. But I wasn't simply made aware of Attea's[21] brokenness and my opportunity to recklessly love her. I was made
aware of the fact that somewhere in the journey of who I was
a year ago to who I am today, I have become not only angry,
but judgmental.

As much as I detest those who cast judgment, stereotypes, and
misconceptions my way, I sure do an awful lot of the same
myself. I may not turn my nose up at the prostitute, the beggar, the homosexual, the divorce, but I immediately and intentionally despise the 'fundies.' I walk into a Christian/Baptist/
Evangelical Free/etc. church and immediately tense up. I in-
stinctively assume the worst. I assume ignorance, close-mind-
edness, judgment, and superiority. And I am wrong to do so,
just as I was wrong to immediately despise the woman with the
bulletins at Thorncrown.

I am grateful to be learning courage. I am coming to find freedom in expressing myself and my beliefs and who I am and
what I know regardless of what others may think of me. The
challenge comes in ensuring I continue to do so regardless of
what others think and not *in spite of.* Sometimes I find myself
becoming so frustrated with things and ideals and traditions
that in an attempt to think freely and avoiding such 'brain-
washing' I instead find myself becoming bitter, cynical, and
calloused to churchgoers and 'Christians' as a whole.

What I didn't mention about Samuel and Joseph[22] is that they
were two of the kindest strangers I have ever spoken to. And

---

21   Name of the woman I encountered on Dickson Street
22   Fundie sign-holders on Dickson Street

why was I so shocked? Because I had assumed the worst. I expected hatred and condemnation to drip from their alcohol-free tongues. And instead? Calm, sure serenity. Disagreement—but acceptance, nonetheless.

I never want to become so damaged that I go through life convinced I am living a radical, free-spirited life of my own making but in reality doing, thinking, and being things just to spite those I feel have hurt me most—the Christians—or whoever else.

There is a fine line between living *deliberately* and living *spitefully* and I hope to never cross it.

Adult Unit

4:00p.m.

Tonight I am working in the adult unit. My very first adult psychiatric hospital experience. I've heard this unit is a breeze because all of the patients are so heavily medicated they just walk around like zombies most of the time. I had never worked the adult unit and have been interested in seeing legitimate 'crazies' as opposed to poorly disciplined children whom as far as I was concerned, had no real issues aside from lack of a leather belt and a lesson in hygiene and respect.

Everyone's eyes are glazed and empty. Except for Diana. For some reason hers are still very much alive. Ironic, as she is the oldest patient present by at least ten years.

Smoke break.

We all trudge to the fenced in patio and I hold up my hand to block the wind while the patients light up. They talk about how they wish they were in the sun –and not the shaded patio. It is thirty-nine degrees outside.

Lydia realizes if she stands right up against the fence and tilts her face upward her nose up to her forehead will be sun soaked as she sucks on her comfort smoke.

I watch her, and my gaze trails upward to the top of the fence, and then behind, where a well-fed robin sits atop a young bare maple.

Free Bird.

He sings down at them and wonders why they are fenced and he is not and continues to give what he can . . . a Hope Song.

I am finished watching Free Bird. His freedom makes me ache for the caged crazies. Instead I peer into the window of the geriatric unit. Leo still wanders the halls aimlessly just as he was over an hour ago. He keeps going back to the same exit door and reaching for the handle six inches left of where the handle is actually situated. The door is locked anyway.

No chance of escape.

Christine in her horizontally red and white striped shirt brags a gold wedding band and I wonder where her husband is—if he is well or passed and what their life was like back when they were riding the Ferris wheel at the county fair sharing a blue cotton candy.

Arnold rises from his apple juice snack at the circle table and begins to strip down in front of everyone. First his shirt, then tie, then the unbuttoning of his pants . . . Samantha (staff) walks briskly over and wraps her arms around his wiry, wrinkled frame. She buttons his pants and guides him to his bedroom.

6:35p.m.

Halfway through dinner and visitation now. Some have visitors and some do not. Janie sits directly in front of me, with Mom and Dad. She is the youngest on our unit now—21 years old. Dad asks me if they are allowed to bring Janie toothpaste.

"Yes sir," I say.

"Janie—what kind do you want—anything but Oral B?"

After they decided on toothpaste Dad asks if he should go ahead and ask Father Thompson to come visit. She is undecided.

Barbara sits by the window with Mom and Pastor. She is just a bit older than Janie and when mom hugged her hello Barbara did not let go for quite a long time. Mom leans forward one hand on chin, "It's hard . . ." Pastor sits cross-legged, hands folded on the square green linoleum cafeteria table. He is bald with glasses and thoughtful. Now he talks with his hands. It is his turn to convince her this is all okay.

Diana sits to the right of me. She rocks a robin's egg blue fitted sweat suit. Her hair is almost GI-Jane short. It is light gold and silver and at least 67 years old she has such a pretty face and bright eyes. Her brother and mother sit with her. Their conversation is easy and laughter is common. They rarely stop smiling and every once in a while brother turns around to check on me. Mom has Alzheimer's. But she is not hospitalized. Her daughter, Diana is.

I'm okay. My eyes smile back at him.

I try to have a cup of Sprite with my chicken-pot-pie dinner but the only thing I tasted is carbonated, stale water. I'm sorry you have to eat and drink here.

Every day.

Paul and Leo and Cynthia go back to the unit. No one came to see them.

Mary enjoys her dinner in the staffing room with her camo-clad army husband, two sons and one daughter—all under the age of 12 years. Mary asks about the cats. Son #2 spins aimlessly in his black leather swivel chair. He is absent and Mary pretends not to notice.

Dad just left Janie and Mom to have some one on one time. It's probably the best.

Five more minutes of visitation. Then back to the unit.

Diana's brother turns to talk to me before he and mom leave. "You look just like my niece—the eyes, your little square nose—just like her." It was comforting go know that's why he kept gazing at me so intently throughout the evening. He had a calm and kind demeanor and his features were strong.

Good man. He loves his sister.

8:46p.m.

Little Red Riding Hood is sitting in a chair across from me in the Day Room as I write. She wears a red fleece blanket over her head and wrapped around her shoulders constantly. Rocking incessantly back and forth she chants, "Stay still. Stay still. Stay still." Earlier she grabbed my hand and ran her nails across it—"Did scratchtht? Need them nail clipperzzzz. See??" The other patients call her "the crazy one." In a psych hospital.

Derek is still on the phone. He clutches his icebreaker mints canister in his hand. The stickers are peeled off. He keeps it in his pocket and takes it out every five minutes to spit in it as if he is enjoying a dip.

No dip.

But it fills the left breast pocket of his denim jean jacket anyway.

Little Red Riding Hood wants me to feel her teeth. "They'rrrre sharp." My ID picture doesn't look like me she says. My hair was long then. I ask her if I should grow it back. Yes, she says. Next time she sees me it better be long.

Mary made me tea. It's Lipton and it's not so delicious. Especially with the very un-natural/organic honey condiments. But still. It's hot and it's caffeine and it is good to the body walking the cold hallways on my 14th hour.

9:55p.m.

Smoke break #3. It's freaking cold outside. I just lit a community cigarette in attempt to keep warm.

Done.

Disgusting. Lorane will finish it for me. She takes it out of the ashtray and re-lights. Everyone thanks me when I hold open the door. It's nice of them.

Back in the Day Room some of the ladies sit and color. I stand, balancing on one hip, flipping the paperwork on my clipboard. Observing. Little Red Riding Hood watches me intently and talks endlessly to me. What? Say again? One more time. And finally, in a very matter of fact tone,

"I DON'T KNOW WHAT YOU ARE SAYING." Lydia and Grace burst into third grade smiles. It's about time someone shut her up.

One more hour . . .

Jacob just arrived. He is a new admit fresh off the streets. Probably fresh off the farm. I follow him to his room and watch him sit on the edge of the bed picking at his fingers. He wears dark leather cowboy boots, Wranglers, and a blue and green plaid button-down shirt. A black Bible sits on his night stand and a cane rests on the wall. His lower back is enveloped by a quite uncomfortable-looking back brace. I wonder what happened. I want to go in and sit on his bedside with him and just have a chat. I think that is against protocol. He seems the kindest one here so far. "Hello there Miss." He saw me watching him. Now I want to talk with him even more so than before—"Miss"? He is a true country gentleman, I am sure of it. I will wait until smoke break and catch him in the hallway. . . We talk of his back pain and his chicken farm and how he has already had two back surgeries to remove numerous back 'spurs' and such.

Jacob looks oddly familiar. Much like a co-worker I used to work with at the Children's Home. They could be brothers. And Little Red Riding Hood strangely resembles my aunt.

I just stepped over to the Geri unit to try out their upright piano. I wanted to see if it was in tune so I could come back during the day and play for the residents, but the nurse on unit shut me up.

"Oh nooononononono—I don't want anyone waking up."

The keys are barely breathing. I go to the freezer and find cotton candy ice cream comfort food. Five minutes to go.

10:45p.m.
Written on the front of my clipboard in black *Sharpie* I find:

"IF GOD BRINGS YOU TO IT—

HE'LL BRING YOU THROUGH IT."

I wonder if they know.

Cardboard Beggar

The other day I realized the reason I don't seem to have much to write about lately is because I haven't had many inter-actions. I started writing this book while in Uganda, East Africa. And while in Uganda, every day presented something I had never before experienced. Every time I set foot out-side our iron-gated home I was sure to meet someone I had never met, and be intrigued by my surroundings. Simply tak-ing a taxi-van ride to Kampala was an experience in itself—crammed 18 people high in a mini-van, with a live chicken at my feet. There was also the chance of running into Natasha the prostitute at John's Shop; and as usual, receiving at least few a marriage proposals a day.

That's not so much the case here in Fayetteville, Arkansas. The 'craziest' thing I've seen lately was a girl giving away at-home-abortion kits (wire hangers) on the street corner. Actually, that was quite a crazy experience. But the point is, that is not the norm. The norm is crawling out of bed after hitting snooze for the seventh time, going to a job I have finally learned to tolerate, and working among people who, for the most part, are much like myself. White, 20's-30's, middle-class.

The norm here in northwest Arkansas is living amongst a population of 75% college kids, at least half of whom have their nose pierced, the vast majority of whom all wear *TOMS**. I think I've seen seven African-Americans since I've lived here. Seven. I realize you may think that is an exaggeration, but I assure you, it is not. And let's not forget, I just spent six months in Africa. Seven is a very small number.

The point is that encountering out-of-the-ordinary people, (or simply, different than myself people) and experiencing out-of-the-ordinary things, is not so easy here. I can't just walk outside onto a red dirt road, cross the trash heap and the Angola cow with horns larger than my body, pass the witch doctor's home, and have a chat with an eight year old Ugandan girl who would like to sell me a bag of peanuts for 25 cents in order to feed her family. Here in northwest Arkansas, life doesn't just happen that way, and people don't just force their way into my day. I can't wait for those crazy-random interactions anymore. I have to go find them.

So in an attempt to create interactions, meet random new people, and in turn have experiences to write about, I began intentionally creating as much human interaction as possible. Rather than use the self-check-out lane at Wal-Mart, I went to a line with a cashier even if the line was 20-people long. Rather than use an ATM at the bank, I used the drive-thru so I would have to talk to a teller. Rather than rent CDs at the library through the automated rental I checked them out from the librarian herself—who looked at me as though I were clearly on all kinds of drugs.

When I paid for gas, I pre-paid inside with cash rather than outside with a debit. These interactions were all well and good—I smiled and asked deep and probing questions such as "How are you?" and, "So is your shift almost over?" But I simply wasn't getting what I wanted. All these interactions were short-lived, and I wasn't exactly getting the eye-opening experiences I need to have in order to write.

I tried to keep my eyes peeled for characters—characters in this book—in this story of life. And low and behold, I found a character indeed.

I was driving down Highway 71 the other day headed towards Springfield for a David Bazan show. I had told a friend I would meet him there around 11:00 a.m. but unfortunately for both of us, I didn't actually wake up until 10:00 a.m.. I finally got on the road and made it to the Missouri border around noon. And what did I see upon entering Missouri? Why, a street corner beggar, of course!

Cardboard Beggar was standing at the intersection of Highway 71 and Commercial directly in front of the Walmart Supercenter. She was looking quite homely, dressed in plaid flannel pajama bottoms, slip-on sandals with socks, and a faded, frayed black hoodie.

"MOM OF 3 KIDS- NO JOB- NEED FOOD AND MONEY."

I read her sign and kept driving . . .for about fifteen yards. And then I pulled over and turned around. I weaved in and out of traffic pondering what exactly was the safest way to stop and talk to Cardboard Beggar. I decided on pulling onto the shoulder right at the corner where she stood, and as I put my car in park, I thought aloud to God,

"I'm not entirely sure what I'm doing. If You have any ideas, please let me know."

I checked the traffic and hopped out of my car, scuttling across the road to Cardboard Beggar. I was headed to Springfield, MO for a lunch date and a concert so I was a bit dressed up. I wondered at how odd the picture was. Me in my boots and skinny jeans and big hoop earrings, all made up for a night on the town—approaching a woman the same age as myself, on a street corner, in pajamas and a hoodie and matted hair, begging for food.

I said 'hello' and asked if I could take her grocery shopping, to which she quickly and eagerly agreed.

The conversation all happened so naturally. It was almost awkward it was so natural—as if the both of us went grocery shopping together on a daily basis. I parked my car and spotted her in the parking lot, then ran up alongside her and we walked in together. I pushed the cart while she picked out food—only the essentials—a loaf of bread, a package of lunchmeat, a bottle of juice, a gallon of milk, a box of cereal. She was conservative with her selections; I wanted to just take over and put half the store in our cart because I was so impressed she wasn't taking advantage of my generosity.

Cardboard Beggar and I talked about her family—a nine-year old boy and a two and a three-year old girl. We talked about how she got where she was, how she and her husband had both recently been laid off from GLAD and were now unemployed and broke.

I purchased Cardboard Beggar's groceries, convinced her to splurge with my money and get a pack of trident gum, gave her $20 cash, and asked if she would mind if I said a prayer with her before I took off. She thanked me profusely, agreed to the prayer, and I left Malynda, with her name and phone number on my Wal-Mart receipt in hand.

It was quite the unexpected feeling I had as I walked back to my car. Because there was no feeling. While walking I fully expected some deep emotion to well up in me—, because I had been the 'Good Samaritan.' I expected to cry, to start pondering deeply the meaning of life. Perhaps to turn around and give her my credit card and all my belongings (which happened to be in my car at the time). But none of that happened. I got in my car, turned on my music, sent a text to my friend telling him I would be even later, and I drove.

And then, a mere five minutes later, the break down happened. I thought about Cardboard Beggar and her sign and her kind eyes and her gratitude and how she did not make the slightest attempt to take advantage of me or my kindness. Mostly I thought about what she said about the church when I asked her if she considered asking them for help. She said she "didn't know they did stuff like help people." And I thought about how it was illegal to beg in northwest Arkansas. I thought about how she was kicked off her street corner in Rogers and told she needed to cross the state line in order to beg. I wondered what she must have felt when one of the only people to stop and talk to her was a cop telling her she couldn't ask for help there—that she needed to go elsewhere.

I thought, for that first five minutes as I left Cardboard Beggar, that I had escaped untouched. I thought to myself, "Wow—I am getting better at this. Not only was it a natural instinct to stop and help, but I didn't even get emotionally involved." That was the goal. That was 'success' for me. To love someone, to reach out to the margianalized and to make an impact—to leave *untouched*.

That is why she is "Cardboard Beggar" and not "Malynda." And that is why Tyler was "Hanger Girl" and Hector was "Mohawk Boy." Because I allowed the hangers and the hawk and the cardboard sign to define them. Wire hangers and crazy hair and cardboard are much less personal than names. There is no attachment there, no commitment to care.

And I got to thinking, perhaps that is what keeps us from talking to Hanger-Girls and Mohawk Boys and Cardboard Beggars. Perhaps it is not simply that approaching strangers, social outcasts, and enemies, is uncomfortable or frowned upon.

It may be that all those things hinder us; but I think most of all, our fear is that *we* will be touched. That we will reach out to hurting people assuming we are their savior, only to realize we are the ones being saved. From complacency, from indifference, and mostly, from calloused hearts.

Our fear is that even if we have the courage to approach the street corner beggar, we do not have the courage to bear the pain we may feel on their behalf as we walk away. Or even worse—we may not be able to forget them.

But I would challenge you to go ahead and touch them anyway.

Notes from Korea (and beyond):

On Loving Self

Earthworm God

I grew up with an egg-God. Three parts in one. God is an egg. He is one being, one thing. And yet somehow, there are three distinct parts. God the Father is the shell. Jesus is the white, and the Holy Spirit is the yoke. Or however you want to phrase it. The point being that He is three in one. The "Trinity." He has also been referred to as apple-God. God the Father is the skin. Jesus is the white fruit, and the Holy Spirit is the seed.

I'm not so sure about egg-apple God. I'm sure about God. It's taken me quite a while but I'm sure about Him. It's the idea of the Trinity I'm not so sure about. I realize that "we" created the heavens and the earth[23]. I know the scripture claims that God always was, He eventually sent Jesus, and Jesus then sent the Holy Spirit. But the egg-God always was three parts. He was always three distinct parts and then He was separated. But still, three *distinct* parts.

What if He wasn't always three distinct parts? What if He was

---

23   In Genesis chapter one the voice of God speaks as "We" and not "I."

one distinct thing—one distinct being, and He didn't become three parts until necessary. What if He was always *just* God. Not God the Father, the Son and the Holy Spirit waiting to separate.

Just God.

What if He was just God for all of time and the post-Creation era, and then one day He decided to *become* two separate parts. Two parts. Not three, two. What if He was just-God forever and ever, and then He formulated this idea to redeem all mankind by sacrificing someone important, but He didn't really have anyone important enough, so He decided the most important and pure being He could possibly sacrifice—was Himself. So just-God sort of split and became not-just-God, but God *and* Jesus.

Jesus-God stayed on earth for a time, did what He had to do, and then realized it might be wise to leave some sort of conscience with his new followers. But how would this be done?! How about splitting Himself *three* ways rather than just two, and becoming a Spirit, in addition to God and Jesus-God.

Brilliant!

So now what was once just-God, is now God, Jesus-God and Spirit of God. Three distinct parts that were once one distinct being. Not an egg. An egg was *always* three parts. It is merely separated when the time comes. An earthworm, however, is an entirely different story. An earthworm is *just* and earthworm. It is *one* earthworm. It is *one* being. It is *one* part. And eventually, when Jr. comes along and decides it is more conducive to chop earthworm into three parts for live fishing bait rather than have just one worm, earthworm becomes three. But earthworm wasn't *always* three parts. He became three parts when it was necessary. First one part, then two, then three.

Perhaps earthworm-God is omniscient and knew all along that He would eventually be three parts and not simply one. Perhaps this is why the scripture states that from the beginning of creation, "We" created the heavens and the earth. Because although at the time of Creation, earthworm-God was *just*-God and not three distinct beings, He knew all along that one day, He would be.

Egg-God.

Apple-God.

Earthworm-God.

This could all be needless banter. This could all be a bunch of seemingly mindless rambling that makes no sense and probably never will. This could be me, questioning the way things are, the way things were, the way things always may have been. It could be me challenging the ideologies I grew up with, the concepts I was spoon-fed while others assumed I would swallow willingly and never regurgitate. Or it could be me sitting in my dungeon-like apartment in South Korea, wondering about God. Wondering who He is, how He is, what He was or how He became. Wondering if we've been right all along with our universally-accepted-by-Christians ideas of the Trinity—the egg-God. Knowing these intricate details may not even matter. In fact, I would venture to say they don't.

But I am recognizing that deliberately *wondering* is always a very good thing.

Jupiter Class

"We do not yell in the classroom! We do not argue! We do not fight! We do not hit each other! WE do not pick our noses! We sit nicely! Stop touching her! Please don't scratch him! NO ARGUING! STOP WHINING!"

I think that pretty much sums up my morning kindergarten classes at Kid's Club in Sangnamdong, Changwon, South Korea. I always thought I loved children—*a lot*. In fact I wanted to have ten of my own. But then I worked in a mental health therapeutic day treatment and hospital for two years with children that pulled my hair, threw desks and chairs at my head, kicked, punched and bit me. One child purposefully vomited onto my new shoes, and several others daily cursed me out. Logic dictates that due to these traumatic experiences, I would never work with children again, especially in a classroom setting.

But they're not mentally unstable. I told myself. *They come from good homes, good families. They are all wealthy and well educated. These kids will be better. This will be . . . different.*

Different indeed. My kids do come from wealthy, well-educat-ed families. They do not vomit on me. They do not curse at me and pull my hair. I have not had to dodge a single flying object yet. For the most part, they actually enjoy learning and crave knowledge—an idea seemingly lost in the United States.

Although the Korean students seem to easily take the cake when comparing behavior and general willingness to learn, they are definitely no angels either. They may not be violent, but they are absolutely entitled. They may not be physically abusing me, but they hit, scratch, grab, and degrade each other every day.

It is the ultimate sin to be less intelligent than others in the classroom. To be so is to guarantee constant humiliation. Sometimes, they are pleasant. They can at times be witty and even entertaining. But mostly I am annoyed. I can't understand why they are not silent when I am speaking and why they are not sitting as still as statues for hours on end. I don't get why they seem to lack respect both for each other and for myself. I cannot comprehend why they find it so necessary to constantly beat one another down physically and verbally.

What kind of people act this way toward one another any-way? I certainly never look out for my own interests before oth-ers. Never do I feel entitled to a well-paying job, a nice home, name-brand clothes, and the latest iPhone. I don't remember ever throwing a punch at a sibling or a friend. I do not fill my mind with constant noise and chatter so I may not hear my God speak . . .

Or do I . . .

———⚫———

Grieving, as it turns out, is a universal language. So is laughter. But today I witnessed the former. Five-year- old Daisy was by far the favorite student in all of Kid's Club Fun Languages English immersion school. She was in Kimberly Teacher's[24] kindergarten class. I didn't ever teach her directly but I saw her every single day in the hallways. I saw her in her giant red, sequin bow headband and her enormous, frilled, poofy dresses. I saw her with her constant smile.

Every day or so I asked, "Hey Daisy, how are you?" And every time she responded, "I'm super duper!" with the most purely joyous, toothy smile you've ever seen.

Daisy *was* super duper.

She's not super duper anymore. Now she is lying in a hospital somewhere in Changwon—lifeless. Why? Because she was so thrilled to see her 12-year-old brother David across the street she ran to him before looking for cars. A van hit her, and then ran over her. I'm sure David saw the whole thing.

David.

David whom I teach every day. David whom Daisy completely adored. David whom she died for. David whom is probably struggling to justify every single breath he takes right now. David who, until today thought Daisy was often an inconvenience.

---

24   In Korea, teachers are addressed by their first name followed by the title 'Teacher'

My kids are an inconvenience. They're an inconvenience when they're picking their nose every second of the day and then touching me with their grimy fingers. They're an inconvenience when they're constantly whining and grunting and yelling and screaming. They're an inconvenience when they only say "more" and never "thank-you." They're an inconvenience when they disregard me entirely because they believe themselves superior to me.

What if it was one of *my* students that were crushed by that van?

I wonder if they would still be inconvenient.

Annyeong

Last night in the shower I had a conversation with God.

I want to believe, I said. *I mean, I want to want to believe. I believe in You. I know you are there. You have to be. I've already tried to believe otherwise and it didn't work.*

Insert a glance to my left wrist, reading and quickly contemplating the "The Hope" written in permanent ink there. Inked at a time when I was sure.

But I'm not so sure about everything else. I'm not so sure about the Bible. I don't get it. I don't understand it. I'm not sure of the details. It bothers me that so many people are convinced the details are important. I don't think they are. I think that it all comes down to seeking Truth. That's it. If we seek, we'll find it, yes? You said that, after all. I think it's okay if we don't get the details right. What frustrates me is that it seems most people—most Christians rather—wouldn't agree.

To be honest, I'm not sure what 'the details' are. I'm not sure they can be put into words, except maybe in bits and pieces throughout this manuscript. Some of you know. Some of you understand.

Right now I'm sitting on my hand-me-down couch in my studio apartment in downtown Sangnamdong, Changwon, South Korea. My studio apartment the size of my living room back in the States. I am listening to a genius mix made from Blue October's "Into the Ocean." A can of grapefruit makgeoli rice wine sits on my hand-painted-by-seven-ex-patriats coffee table. I am sporting a gray and hot pink, child's fleece monkey hat the school gave to me rather than donating it to the trash bin. My laundry sits in piles on the chair, the drying rack, the floor, my bed post, and the washing machine.

This is my life in Korea.

⸺⸱❦⸱⸺

Arrested Development may very well be the best TV show ever made. If you disagree, that is okay, but you are wrong. There is an adopted brother on the show whose name is "Annyeong", which is hilarious because translated it simply means "Hello." So, whenever anyone speaks his name on the show the subtitle text reads "Hello." When I first came to Korea, I remember hearing "Annyeong" for the first time and of course immediately thinking of *Arrested Development*. It had a whole new firsthand meaning to me now. But the more I heard the word, the sooner I came to realize 'Annyeong' was simply a shortened version of "Annyeong Hasayo," which is the entire, proper way to say hello.

Even more recently—a couple of weeks ago in fact—I learned the literal translation is not, in fact, "Hello," but rather, "Are you at peace?" This would explain why when responding to the greeting Koreans don't simply repeat the phrase, but first answer "Naay", and then repeat the phrase.

They are answering the question, you see. "Yes, I am at peace. Are you at peace?"

I am not at Peace.

Not at this moment, and not most of the time. I attribute this not to where I live on my ten hour work days nor my seemingly constant allergen attacks. I attribute this to myself and my unwillingness to stop, to listen, to breathe—to simply, be still.

I want to know that He is God. I want to know and be sure, beyond doubt. The problem is that in order to know, I have to *be still*. Peace comes only during stillness, and knowing follows.

Annyeong haseyo?

Let Us Eat Cake

The pieces of Korea I treasure most are the unplanned ones. The weekend trips and tour-bus ventures, the holiday getaways specifically catered to tourists, the temple stays and meals—all of these pre-packaged, tourist and foreigner-friendly escapades leave something to be desired.

My favorite moments in Korea consist entirely of unexpected, unplanned, candid interactions with locals.

I once shared my birthday cake with the middle-aged, silver-haired, valet man and he smiled so greatly and was so genuinely appreciative that I continued onward toward our cell phone store[25] and sat down to have cake with the owner, his employee, his wife and her friend.

This happened about three months into my year teaching contract in Korea. One of my students brought me a coffee-flavored birthday cake for my birthday, but because he was angry

---

25   I used a cheap, pay-as-you-go flip phone in Korea, paying only about $5.00 every week for pay-as-you-go service.

with the other students in the class, he decided that I was not to share the cake but must bring it home and enjoy it without them.

I opened the cake in the teacher's room and upon realizing it was delicious, also realized that it was entirely to rich for me to finish on my own. I shared it with my coworkers who were more than happy to partake, but still had half of a coffee-flavored birthday cake leftover.

What to do . . .

While walking home cake in hand, Tim and I bowed to the valet man who works at the restaurant next door to our apartment building and gave him the usual greeting. And then, I had a grand idea.

"Let's give him cake!" I said to Tim.

He was puzzled.

"Well, we happened to have this clean bowl in hand from earlier this morning, we have way too much cake, and why not share?

So we did.

We shared my cake. And valet man wore a grin so huge I just couldn't help but think to walk down the street to our cell phone store and share it there as well. The owner's wife happened to be present that day. And his wife's friend, and his employee of course.

"Cake?" I asked. "My birthday! Do you want some cake?"

There was only a millisecond of complete befuddlement before the owner nodded, "Yes!" and scurried to find Dixie cups to serve the cake in since we had no plates, or utensils, or napkins.

So we ate cake.

Tim, myself, the owner, his wife, his employee, his wife's friend. We sat around a bright white table at the cell phone store and ate coffee birthday cake. Out of Dixie cups. With our hands.

And for the fist time since living in Korea—I loved Korea. For the first time in three months, I understood how someone could fall with this culture—these people.

Before this I had not yet experienced Korean kindness. I had experienced being invisible. I had experienced being ignored. I had experienced nearly being run over.

Every.

Single.

Day.

But this? This sitting with, eating with, devouring cake with Korean locals? This was new. And this I loved.

The only words spoken during this cake feast were "Thank you" and "delicious". The rest was a mad mixture of charades, body language, and guessing. But not many words are really necessary at such a scene. Kindness is understood. Generosity is appreciated. Thankfulness is shown. And who doesn't love coffee flavored birthday cake?

Koreans are generally quite kind. They are thankful, they are warm, they are generous, and they are respectful. They are also not ever going to be the first to make a move. (Unless they are a drunken businessmen post-soju). They simply will not be.

It took one move. It took one idea. It took one small effort to reach out and touch them rather than waiting sulkily to be touched to experience the beauty of this culture.

How many times have I missed out on such opportunities here, in the states, anywhere—because I was waiting for the other to make the first move?

And so, in the spirit of Korea—let us eat cake.

Korea

Korea, you are breaking me
Korea, I am allergic to your air
You bury me alive in thick, polluted haze
Korea, you make me gasp for breath I cannot find
You wretched place, you life-sucking, almost island
You sorry excuse for a country
I do not understand you
And again
I do not understand you

Korea, you have driven me to sobriety
You offer cheap vodka-juice
And piss-water beer
With a side of drunk men
Vomiting
In the streets
Every night

Yet . . .

You're crawling with children
Speaking two languages better than I speak one
Knowledge seeps from your odorless pores
You who wear no deodorant
Korea, You inspire me
With your hard work
Your drive
Your slow climb
Back to the world
After. . .

Japan

Look at you
So eager to utilize your new tongue
You put 'English' on every notebook, pencil, coffee cup,
restaurant
It doesn't make sense
"At Home Safety Kitchen"?
Every time it brings a smile
And a gutteral chuckle
"Oh Korea" I say
Oh
Korea

You feel so emotionless
Sometimes, so obsessed with everything you are not
Your eyes will never grow
Nor your neck
Nor lashes

And yet—resilient!

I go to your markets and find the biggest thrift store I've
ever seen!
Sweaters, suede, shoes, belts, bags, blankets
Anything and everything
Three dollars
With your ajumma telling me
As I try on a dress
"Oh beautiful! Movie star!"
Mmmm-yes

Your starless sky has parched my soul
Your fireworks helped to ease the pain
A finale over an hour long!
Well done
Well
Done

Korea how do you have so many festivals
Kimchi
Hot Air Balloon
Cherry Blossom
Chocolate
Ice
Snow
Music
Mask
Trout
Persimmon
Festival

I will never accept your six dollar drip brew
But I thank you for your six coffee shops
On each
Block

I will never love your never-ending apartments
Your stacked city
Your marble hallways echoing
The prostitutes' heels

But I thank you for
Your surrounding mountains
Your ocean
Your yellow trees that refuse to fall
When autumn is so far gone
So far
Gone

I will never accept your kimchi
That rotted, spice cabbage
That twisted idea of overmedicated 'health'
Your sugared garlic toast is a
Sick joke

But I thank you for endless
Garlic
Pork
Beef
Sautéed onions
GRILLED
On fresh lettuce
$6

Korea why do I fear death every time
I walk
On your filthy streets
Your careless scooters almost kill me
Every
Time

On the bus, in the taxi, on the road
I always say,
"Life. Are you still here?"
And now, still?

Korea your cross-country buses
How they put Greyhound to shame
To
Shame!
And for fifty dollars only
From border to border

I do not appreciate your
Incessant
NOISE
Your prostitute's heels
And quarrels echoing through the concrete halls

But "GOOOOD MORNINGGGGGG AMYROSE
TEACHER!!!!!"
I do not mind
I will never mind

And some days I wonder
If I may miss that howling dog
That screeching cat
That domestic fight
Every
Night

I catch a smile creeping
Across my face
As the neighbor begins his hideous cackling
That so many nights keeps me awake
These sounds are

HOME

I do not appreciate your shove
On the subway
The bus
In line
The bathroom
The street

But I thank you for your bow
Young child
Mother
Stranger

I refused to learn your alphabet
I force you to learn mine

Korea, always you surprise me
I cannot hate you
Every time I try to, you love me
In some illogical Korean way
In return

Korea
Nice-uh

Elephants, Ganges, Taj & Stench

India is nothing that I thought it would be. Hollywood makes it look like all painted elephants, festival of color, beautiful cloths, countless temples—the world famous Taj Mahal. The reality is that India is one over-populated and never-ending heap of trash with a few beautiful temples here and there, perhaps lot of temples, but not enough to balance out the trash and filth.

I was told the air would smell of Indian curry sweat. Instead my nostrils are permeated by the scent of thick, dehydrated urine.

I have not seen a single painted elephant.

I have seen more dogs (all stray mutts—most pregnant) in one week than I have in my entire life. There are no Korean ajummas[26] here. The trash does not disappear by 9 o' clock in the morning. It only continues to accumulate.

---

26   In Korea, older women called "ajummas" were responsible for cleaning the streets and
       sorting the trash early in the morning before 9a.m.

And yet, still India is beautiful. Just in an entirely different way than I expected to find.

The most breathtaking thing I've seen thus far is not the flawless Taj nor the holy Ganges or the markets and bazaars of endless color, but the faces of the slum children. How their dark eyes light up at our very presence. The Indian women's constant smiles given almost every time eye contact is made. A smile given means a smile returned. And even the beggars. How is someone so beaten and broken, so filthy and ragged, still so stunningly beautiful?

The best smile I've seen so far came from a 10-year-old street boy begging for rupees. Instead we gave him leftover naan. His response was not rejection, nor asking for more, but thanking, smiling, and walking away.

If I could give a smile such as he had to a single soul every day, I think my life would be well spent. But then, it is easy to feed the beautiful beggar children of India every couple of days. It is not so easy to offer such hope and sustenance daily in the States, where I am not a movie star[27] American and will not receive endless thanks.

I hope I will love you, white, middle-class American—you who do not make me look like a saint. I cannot take my picture with you and appear a world-traveling life-giver.

But I hope to love you anyway.

---

27   Foreigners, Americans especially, in India are somewhat revered in India. We are looked at as "movie stars" in a way.

Bugs & Beaches

Sometimes I think of religion as a sort of beach bug.

Here I am lying on the beach of life. The sun is shining, the waves are crashing, I am tanning, but then there is this ridiculously annoying beach fly constantly landing on my calves and feet. I feel like a cow or horse suddenly—switching my tail (or feet) every few seconds to force the flies to get off and away. But I can't ignore them; they are there. And although the beach is glorious, the fact is that it is not altogether perfect. Sometimes the sun burns. The sand can yield hard and even sharp objects painful to walk on. The tide can swallow my book and towel before I can even know it is coming.

It is not, altogether, perfect.

And the insects are always there. Whether some species of gnat, fly, mosquito, or ant, they are there. And no matter how much I swat and huff and puff, they are not going to go away.

That is, as of late, how religion seems to me. It doesn't go away.

Sometimes it is more obvious and present than other times, but it always *is*.

Whether Christianity (one of the 50,000 + brands therein) in America, Buddhism in Korea, Hindu/Muslim/Buddhism in Thailand—it is ever present. I can't get it to go away. I've tried.

Life without God, to me, is life without Hope. And to me, that is not a life worth living.

A dear friend (and atheist) once argued, "Religion is a crutch. That is all." At the moment her statement took me aback. Later, I agreed with it. And finally, I embraced it.

I later told her, "If Christianity is a crutch,then fine. It is one I am openly and willingly leaning on. I tried to live without it and I simply cannot."

Someone once told me, "If you're standing in a place and every-one around you is screaming at the top of their lungs the same [mantra] over and over, eventually, you will come to believe it."

Given time, I must say, I would probably have to agree with this statement. But then that leads me to wonder—am I a Christian because for twenty-two years of my life everyone around me was screaming, "JESUS SAVES!!!!" Are Muslims Muslim because everyone around them is bowing to Mecca and praying to Allah? Perhaps. But then there is my dear friend Fern. The one who said religion is a crutch. The one who is an atheist. The one who grew up with everyone screaming, "JESUS SAVES!!!"

So perhaps it is a choice after all. And maybe the idea of God is similar to a pestering insect because the pestering insect *is*. It will never go away. It will always be. It cannot be erased or obliterated whether or not I choose to believe it's there. The only difference is, the beach pest offers disruption, while God offers *Peace*.

Rooster Riot

I thought that after six months living in Uganda, returning once, and doing humanitarian aid work in El Salvador and Mexico I had seen enough poverty and brokenness to effectively form a calloused heart.

I also thought that roosters at 3 o' clock in the morning were the worst thing that could possibly be outside my window when all I want is sleep.

I was wrong on both counts.

I only *thought* the 3 a.m. rooster was the worst evil because I had not yet endured a hotel room situated directly on the highway and the constant horn blowing of New Delhi traffic.

And I only *thought* a beggar—no matter what age, size, or race could no longer pierce my soul because I had not yet seen Indian children—stroking my arms, all chocolate eyes and wide smiles. I had not yet given them our leftover bread and watched their eyes light up with hope. I wanted to scoop them up and take them with me to the metro.

The thing about those horrid ads on TV is—they're not personal. Do they inflict guilt? Yes, more times than not (while watching from the comfort of my living room couch) they do. But they are also staged, and through a TV screen, and who knows what percentage of the money I send is actually going to those children. TV ads produce guilt. Tiny Indian children offering all smiles—even with empty bellies and matted hair—I'm not sure what it produces. Something deeper than sadness. Something I can't quite express. The kind of feeling you don't want to dwell on long for fear it will change your life, perhaps by forcing you to act.

To love.

Meeting Rahul

Today I met Rahul. He is a young Indian man born and raised in Mumbai but currently residing in Hyderabad. Rahul is a businessman. He is quite tall in stature and also quite stylish. We are smoking hookah with Rahul at a local hookah joint when Rahul decided to tell us his story . . .

"I used to do drugs, you guys. All kinds of drugs—like really bad stuff. One night I stayed out late at a club and came home to crash. When I woke up the next day my house servant saw me and just started crying. She said she thought I was dead. 'Why?' I asked 'I was just sleeping through the night'."

It had been three days. Rahul had slept for 72 hours. He goes on to tell us it was at that point he realized he needed a drastic lifestyle change. He made a decision to follow *Yeshuji*.

In Indian culture it is very acceptable and even encouraged for one to talk about spirituality and religion. The Hindus have 320 million gods so they are able to pick and choose which they would like to worship. They are often very accepting of the idea of Yeshuji—and may even decide to follow Him in addition to the gods they are already following. What they are not okay with is "converting" to Christian culture.

In India, Hindu is more a culture than a religion—and the same goes for Christianity. If you are born into a Hindu family, you are Hindu. If you are born into a Christian family, you are Christian. Hindus represent more traditional Indian culture while Christians represent westernized culture. So many Indians have a very negative perception of Christianity. It means missionaries coming and forcing their western culture upon Hindu India. It means if they want to believe differently, if they want to follow Yeshuji, they must leave their Hindu culture behind.

My friends Jason and Tina are living in India. I am staying with them for a few days. Jason explained to us that due to the negative connotations associated with Christian verbiage such as: *Jesus, disciple, God, Christianity*—when they share the story of Jesus with any Indians the words are changed to more fit their Hindu culture.

Example:

Jesus- *Yeshuji*
Teacher- *Guru*
God- *Bhagwon*
Disciple- *bhakta*
Church- *satsang*

This way the Indians may recognize Yeshuji and choose to

follow without feeling they must give up their entire culture, family and heritage.

So much of the last few years have been spent in question. More and more I have come to believe that anyone who is Christian is only so because it is the most prevalent religion where they reside. I have come to recognize in traveling how large the world is—how many religions, beliefs, peoples and cultures it holds and how very small America is.

I have come to believe that religion is something you come upon according to when and where you are raised, and you embrace it, or you don't. Or you may go back and forth. I have come to realize I am not so sure I can ever fully embrace the *Jesus* I grew up with ever again.

But then I met Rahul.

And he introduced me to Yeshuji. And I think perhaps I could follow *Him*.

A Henna Song

I sit inside a tiny shop in a plastic, dirt-stained lawn chair. Ashita sits on the floor below me, my hand and forearm resting gently on her thigh.

Henna.

Tim looks on in between gaming on his iPhone to pass the time while I indulge. A young boy walks into the shop carrying a tiny bundle. A baby. One month old, all eyes. Ashita stops her work a moment to place her baby in a miniature hammock tied between the legs of the table that holds her jewelry goods. Tim swings the hammock continuously with his index finger while gaming with his free hand.

Henna continues only after I efficiently ooh and ah over the mini-Indian—the smallest one I have seen yet. A beggar comes to the front of the shop. Not uncommon. Street beggars have followed us for quite a distance before. Foreigners, of course, are easy targets. Most of us have not yet been made aware the crippling and long-lasting effects of handouts and foreign aid.

There are three. Mother, five-year-old son and random tag-a-long girl around seven years of age. Although due to malnutrition she is more likely to be 10. The woman has an instrument, if you can call it that. It is a box, almost like a cigar box. She opens it slowly and one long, lingering tune comes forth. One note, one pitch—a sort of—almost a vibration. It is nothing much, just enough o compliment her voice. Smooth, rich, enchanting. I don't know what language. Possibly Hindi. But just as likely one of the thousands of local dialects spoken in this country.

She was singing and hoping. Hoping she may be given 10 RPS (less than one dollar) or so for her song. I stared. Usually I instantly turn away when a beggar comes my way. It may sound harsh and heartless I realize but the fact is I can't feed them all. But this time I stared. Openly and deeply I held her gaze. Her voice was beautiful—mesmerizing.

I wanted her to stay forever.

But when we paid she left, mariachi band style, only singing until paid off. I wanted to get up and chase her down. Tell her if she stayed and sang some more we would double her money or buy her dinner—anything to make her stay and sing.

Her voice. Her musical cigar box. It is the most beautiful thing I have heard in India. It is the most beautiful thing I have heard in a long time. When I leave I want to remember her face and her song rather than the filth and haze and stray dogs and constant honking of horns and badgering of taxi drivers.

She is My India song. She is the voice I will take away and tuck deeply in my memory and hope to stay forever. She is a piece of beauty and peace in a place of filth and ruin.

She is my song.

I wonder if I have ever been someone's song. I wonder if my single, fleeting interaction with a stranger, perhaps a foreigner may have left a lasting piece of Hope in an otherwise dreary place.

I want to be a song.

Tomorrow if I see her on my way to the bus stop I will tell her—"You are my song. You are my beautiful India song in a not very beautiful place. I want to be a song like you."

Notes from St. Louis:

ON LOVING DOUBT

Dumpster Dinners

The other night I went dumpster diving. I had done this in college at the end of the year when the new graduates threw out trashcans, blow driers, lamps, furniture and toiletries galore.

I specifically remember a time when my non-dumpster-diving friends drove into their apartment complex parking lot late one evening only to find my friend Whitney and I entirely *inside* their apartment dumpster, with flashlight and headlamp, wallowing in filth . . . or treasures, rather.

We froze in the glare of their headlights, of their stares, for a moment ashamed--and then quickly soared beyond shame upon remembering what lie below and continued rummaging. Whitney and I were the poorest of our clique, you see. She grew up on government cheese and discount food items from the nearby Native American reservation and I grew up on expired food and 100% garage sale attire. We were the ones working through college. If free goods were to be had, Whitney and I wanted in. So—dumpster-diving.

That was seven years ago. I was 21 years old and in college shopping for free furniture and half- used name brand shampoo. Maybe a full-length mirror if I was really lucky.

This time was different. This time I was 29 years old and rummaging through the cockroach-infested dumpster of an organic food store, in search of groceries for my best friend.

We were looking for *food*. In a *dumpster*.

And while Jade felt right at home and practically dove in headfirst—tearing open bags and slowly becoming covered in grime—I did not.

When I hit the dumpster in college I was shopping for accessories, for whatever was free and looked neat. Most of the good stuff was actually set neatly *outside* the dumpster and anything else was piled in heaps—not hidden beneath the stench of rotting strawberries and greasy mayo. I realized, while in the dumpster, watching the cockroaches, that some people don't do this for fun.

They do it to live.

I don't mind dirt. In fact, one of my favorite past times in all the world is running and playing in the rain and mud. I wait tables. I am covered in sweat and food particles the majority of my shift. I have slept with cockroaches literally as big as my hand crawling the walls of my home in the African heat. I have worked disaster relief jobs that required me to suck raw sewage from carpets with a wet vac. Again, I don't mind dirt.

But this? This was repulsive. The stench. The cockroaches crawling on the food we were picking The cockroaches with which we were trapped inside a six by six foot metal box. The filth on my hands—my face—my clothes—my car. It was truly disgusting.

For some reason I thought dumpster diving would be fun. Maybe that's because in college, it was. We didn't *need* the items we were looking for to survive. We simply wanted them. And they were free.

Dumpster diving this time wasn't about free lamps and apartment accessories. It was about getting free food to be taken home, rinsed off, eaten and stored because food stamp money was running low. And that made me uncomfortable. It made dumpster diving not so fun after all.

Jade, however, seemed to be having a blast. As I said, she dove right in. We went home with two watermelons, a carton of strawberries, a bag of lemons, a box of mushrooms, two eggs, three blueberry scones, several tomatoes, a box of cereal, a zucchini, and three or four not-so-frozen-anymore stir-fry dinners.

She could eat for days.

Really, she had food at home. It may not have lasted long, but it was there. Jade dumpster-diving for her dinner didn't make me uncomfortable. The thoughts the situation provoked did. I thought about all of Jade's California friends, her homeless friends, her wandering friends—who do this not once a month for *extra* food, but every day for *all* their food. I thought about all the starving people in all around the world who don't do this for a 'late night adventure' but rather, simply to survive.

Honestly, this wasn't one of those life-changing moments for me where I realized I needed to 'quit my day job' (that I don't have) and go feed the hungry.

I realized I'm glad I have friends like Jade.

There was a time in my life (age 0-24 years) when almost every person I knew was white, middle-class and conservative Christian. I am entirely grateful for my upbringing and my education and I would not change anything at all given the chance. But sometimes, when I look back and see that, I want to vomit.

I am overwhelmed when I look at my life now, and back at the last five years, and see conversations with bearded homeless men; car rides with hitchhikers and their dogs; art parties in Korea with Americans, Canadians, Christians, Jews; sharing coffee with abortion rights activists; accidentally attending a lesbian beach bonfire (which for the record was maybe the most entertaining and fun bonfire of my life).

I am thankful for these interactions. I am thankful for the 'Nons.' The non-believers. The non-whites. The non-middle-class. The non-'normal.' The dumpster divers.

Because they make me see.

Church Beers

I came to church this morning because I thought it would be good for me. I thought it would be beneficial to be in a place where I knew I would be surrounded by people giving off positive energy and exuding selfless Love. But as I sit in this auditorium I can't help but wonder how much the electric bill is for a place like this. I can't help but stare at the set design trees made of two-by-fours with hanging lanterns—and wonder why it is at all necessary. I can't help listening to sermon #377 on 1 Corinthians 13 and how important it is to LOVE and wonder if anyone will leave this building living Love any differently. I can't help sitting in the high school service and looking around at all the moldable youngsters, wondering if even 10% of them, after going off to college and living in the real world will keep the faith.

The church is not a bad thing—a bad group of people. It can be, yes. But overall I don't believe it is a stain on society and I don't mean to slam places like the place I sit now.

But I do not feel Christian here.

What I mean is that I don't really think that spending an hour or so within church walls listening to the same sermon I've heard for years is a way in which I can most exemplify Jesus.

Yesterday I worked a twelve-hour shift at Little Hills Winery. When it came time to clock out I was beyond ready. I was covered in grime and sweat and completely exhausted. Not too mention a bit smelly. But then my friend Madeline called. She wanted to go for a drink. And because she is absolutely one of my favorite co-workers and because she is in a similar place in life, I decided to go. In my all black skid-proof Dr. Scholl's, messy bun and nasty grimy work attire, complete with Little Hills name tag—I decided to go.

On the patio of Millstream Bar surrounded by Christmas lights and our recent Little Hills' customers, we discussed Life over blueberry ale. We talked of love and loss and hurt and heart-ache and family and childhood and being third-born. We ate a Quik Trip fruity rice krispy treat and doused our bodies in bug repellent and discussed tattoo stories. We rambled about religion or lack thereof and the similarities between our mothers and sisters. We shared shots that tasted like alcoholic mouth-wash and bonded with the bartender over my hideous shoes. We shared art through emails upon our safe arrival home.

For most of my life I thought that Christianity was about con-vincing everyone else that we are right and they are wrong. That there's One Way and it's our way and let us tell you why.

But it's not.

It's about LOVE.

I loved Madeline last night. And I am more than sure Jesus would have been sharing blueberry ale with us if He walked the earth in flesh today. As for sitting through a sermon on Love within a building costing thousands of dollars—I'm not so sure.

But I am sure He would have listened to Madeline's story. And I am sure He would have shared His.

Back to the Lou

There came a point my not so recent past that I found myself in fetal position on my bedroom floor sobbing hysterically, to the point of hyperventilating. For the first time in 26 years, I couldn't cry out to God. I was physically and psychologically incapable of doing so, because I believed with all my heart there was simply no one there. The only thing comparable to that kind of devastation is either a severe break up or the death of a loved one.

I don't know that I have ever felt so alone in my life. It was terrifying, to say the last.

Eventually, I found—or recognized—God again. To be honest, I don't quite remember the details of how. I just remember that living without Him eventually was no longer an option. It was as if my mind had played some sort of trick on me—convincing me that God was either dead, or never was. I just know that condition didn't last long. I was completely incapable of denying Him. I tried. And I failed.

He simply was.
He simply is.

The rest of it? Of faith, of God, of Christ? I'm still attempting to piece it all together. I'm still trying to understand.

Life doesn't make sense. It's not supposed to. If it did, there would be no mystery. It's what keeps us going—trying to understand, even though we never will (in this life). Trying to get it right, but knowing we won't—not yet.

God is usually where we least expect Him—in a birthday card. In the comments of an atheist. In the touch of a yoga instructor. If there's anything I've learned to be absolutely true throughout these years of wandering it is that until I stop expecting to see Him in all the places I was taught to look (churches, Bible studies, 'worship music', etc.) and start remembering to be aware that He is everywhere—I will cease to be moved.

What I can hold on to is the Truth I do know. The Truth I do understand.

The Truth is that I have seen the face of God—in the slum children of Farrhidabad, India. In the homeless beggar man on the streets of New Orleans. In my children at the group home.

The Truth is that the most content, joyful, confident, fearless, and effective I have ever been was when I closely walked with God.

The Truth is that I had a dream to drill a well in Africa. I asked God to make that dream happen and it did. Those children and that village in Entebbe, Uganda will never thirst again.

The Truth is that when I am alone and broken, I find comfort in His name.

Truth does not hide. Is it difficult to find? Sometimes, yes. But it is there for those who want it. It is there for those who cannot help but wonder. Those who cannot help but wonder who God really is, if Jesus really was, how we really are to live.

The Truth is that He is Hope when there is none. He must be.

So I continue to wonder.

*Clara's Creed

Once upon Apache Drive, there was a girl named Clara. Clara was born into a God-fearing family, living in Columbia, South Carolina in a modest, two-bedroom, one bathroom house. Clara was third-born of three, soon to be four children of Jacob and Deborah. Jacob worked full-time while also attending seminary. As money was more than tight, meals often consisted of outdated, stale bread donated from the bread factory, toasted with cheese and declared 'daddy toast.' Bearing such a name brought the stale bread from poor folk grub to a household delicacy.

Summers for young Clara consisted of gathering pecans from the ground in the front yard, splashing in the round, plastic pool in her rainbow swimsuit, and visiting the elderly Miss Hoover down the road, who consistently provided a bowl of chicken flavored Ramen noodles, and an afternoon of playing with colored plastic snap beads. Only on very special occasions, Clara was allowed to walk down the gravel road with her father to pluck cucumbers from the neighbors' garden. This was the highlight of Clara's life, until she was brutally attacked by fire ants one day while doing so.

Growing up in the south was short-lived, as the family relocated to a booming suburb just outside of St. Louis, Mo in order for Jacob to take a job pastoring a small Evangelical Presbyterian church. The family relocated just in time to pop out child number four, and Clara eagerly played the part of a PK[28] dressed in froofy, laced, puff-sleeve dresses and black patton-leather shoes, her cocoa ringlets bouncing, her emerald eyes sparkling.

Clara played the part well, adorable pastor's daughter. She rarely failed to wear a cheeky smile, and was quick to offer a fearless embrace to her favorite members of the congregation, most especially the young high school men, any of whom five-year-old Clara was sure she would marry in a moment's notice if they were to ask.

Sunday morning gatherings held at the local YMCA were always the highlight of Clara's week-they meant admiring her father as he dispersed wisdom to the masses, reveling under the adoring eyes of the congregation, and of course, a plethora of orange juice and donuts after service.

These were the good days. The days which Clara would look back on with great fondness, while wondering at why they were so fleeting. Grace Church EPC only survived for five years, and then the dark day came when the faithful few left in the congregation gathered one last time in the YMCA, and

---

28   Slang for "pastor's kid"

Reverend Thompson uttered such final words as "church is folding . . .thank-you . . .this will be our last meeting . . ."

Young Clara sat upon her elder sister's lap, sobbing, not entirely understanding the cause of the death of the church, but recognizing, nonetheless, this was the end of an era, the end of something she knew to be good, and rare and treasured. After the church's life was severed, Clara's despondent father turned to quite a different career, for a time as a real estate agent, then as a maintenance man, and finally, a career in sales. Clara's mother also dabbled in various jobs, both ensuring all four children attended private, Christian schools K-12 in order to guarantee a well-educated and biblically sound upbringing. Clara memorized entire Psalms in KJV at the age of five years and was well-instructed by both parents in the ways of the scriptures. Although Jacob no longer pastored a church of his own, he still preached from time to time, and young Clara was always impressed with the great wisdom her father had to impart to the crowds of hungry souls.

Debrah also played a vital role in the children's religious upbringing, denouncing such sins as partaking of smoking, piercings, tattoos, lying and voting for democrats. Clara never fought the rigid rules under which she was brought up, knee length shorts only and no 'official' dating until seventeen years of age. She flourished at church youth group.

Clara was more than excited to get out from under her parents' regime and see the world on her own. Her college career was spent at a baptist university in the Ozarks of southwest Missouri, and the summer following graduation she interned at a seminary camp in the heart of New Orleans, where she led teams of high school youth groups in rebuilding the city post-Katrina. When her internship came to an end, Clara found herself back in the Ozarks this time working as a live-in Youth Care Specialist. Clara lived at a therapeutic group home with teenage girls 24/7 every other week. This time was what Clara would later say was the highlight of her life.

Clara grew up believing as her parents had taught her. Although they often encouraged their children to be skeptics, analyzing and weighing all they were told with a microscopic eye, Clara naturally accepted all they had to offer without question, trusting whole-heartedly in their wisdom of age, as well as experience. Clara's creed was not formed entirely by her parents, however. Much of her moral stance and world-view could be attributed to twenty-three years in evangelical Christian churches, as well as twenty-three years of private school education.

As fate would have it, Clara, after returning from a year of teaching ESL abroad, decided to move to Portland, OR where her current boyfriend would be attending grad school in the fall. Clara, a quite independent young woman, was not one to follow any man anywhere, but as she currently had no plans of her own and needed to determine whether or not she would marry the gentleman, she packed her bags and headed west. Clara secured a job at an all-girls boarding school mentoring troubled teens. Clara and boyfriend had lived in Oregon only a few short months when he decided he no longer wanted to be with her.

According to boyfriend, Clara was a restless wanderer bound

and determined to travel the world indefinitely while he was more than ready to 'settle down' and stay in one place forever. Entirely blind-sided, Clara grieved for one full week and then made up her mind to go ahead and continue to stay in Oregon, as she saw no reason to start over yet again now that she had finally secured a job, a church, and a social life.

Clara moved to the town where she worked and eagerly began building her newly single life. In order to take her mind off the fact that she was now alone in a far-off state and had recently been rejected, Clara found various things to do with her time away from work. Mondays were spent teaching art classes to special needs children, Wednesdays Clara played piano for the elderly at the local nursing home and Saturdays were spent camped out at Barnes and Noble, people-watching, writing poetry, and guzzling coffee for hours at a time. When Clara was not busy doing all of the above, she was making music upstairs with her newfound co-worker friend Willow with incense burning and red wine flowing.

Afternoons were often spent falling asleep in Wilson Park while lounging in a hand-woven, El Salvadorian hammock hung neatly over the gurgling creek. While living in Oregon, Clara found herself surrounded by all sorts of people that she had previously not surrounded herself with. For example, she was beginning to form quite close relationships with people whom did not think, breathe, believe and act precisely as she did. Namely, they were not born and bread evangelical Christians. Clara became close to all kinds of rogues—Roman Catholics, Episcopalians, Jehovah's Witnesses, Agnostics. . .democrats, abortion rights activists. Clara noticed her worldviews were beginning to be challenged, as she recognized more and more just how close-minded she had actually become.

One well-read, intellectual friend of Clara's encouraged her questioning nature almost constantly, and slowly Clara began to wonder whether or not she really believed anything she grew up believing at all. Terms such as Trinity, hell, Holy Spirit, pre-destination, virgin birth, and homosexual sin befuddled Clara, and there seemed to be numerous concepts, practices, and terms which were not, in fact, found anywhere in the Bible, but were assumed or created by the church.

And the Bible—the inspired and inerrant Word of God—with-out flaw, without contradiction, the book upon which Clara had formed her unspoken creed, her entire foundation of faith, was now in question as well.

Apparently, there was much about the Bible she was unaware of, such as the fact that Genesis contained not one, but two creation stories, both quite different and both written by entirely different authors. Much of the book was greatly influenced by the current authorities in power at the time of its production and much has been lost throughout the various translations of the manuscript.

As Clara's creed began to dissipate upon realizations that all she thought she knew was concrete, absolute fact was in fact, not, and upon recognizing one did not necessarily have to be a regu-lar attendee of an evangelical Christian church worshiping as she did, believing fact by fact as she did, practicing 'religion' as she did, in order to love God and all He is and live righteously and love people. . .

Clara became overwhelmed with this newfound revelation, and although in part, she felt liberated, she also feared she would somehow lose her salvation—whatever that meant—if she continued allowing her mind to open up to universalist concepts and live accordingly. Clara found that every time she attended her weekly Bible study she found less and less common ground with those who attended, and feeling a bit alienated, decided to no longer attend the study, nor the church with which it was associated. Clara's extra-curricular activities slowly subsided and as the stress level at work began to escalate, she often found herself coming home to drown her troubles in a bottle of Jack she kept conveniently by her bedside, where she frequently drank herself into a deep sleep.

As the dulling effect of the alcohol became less and less by the day, Clara began to find solace in other things, namely ungodly amounts of herb, cutting to revert to physical pain rather than emotional, and most especially, men. Where mind-altering substances failed, the attention, desire, and touch of numerous men quickly and effectively filled the role of pain-dulling and displacing the hopeless reality of current-day life. What first began with flirtatious glances to strangers at the local pub soon became frequent one-night stands. Clara was more than desirable to all men who met her irresistible stare. While she radiated with outward beauty she also presented an aura of pleasant energy and appeal that was indescribable and capable of drawing any man nigh.

One sad day Clara learned she was pregnant by one of her many customers. A man name Linus—47 years old and married with four children. Clara contemplated keeping the baby boy, whom she contemplated naming James. But she opted for an abortion at 21 weeks instead. Linus was pleased, as he feared he may be stuck footing the bill for the bastard. Shortly after the abortion he demanded Clara be tested for STD's, declaring in a matter of fact way to her one day, "I only fuck clean whores."

Clara conceded to his will and soon after wished that she had not upon learning she was HIV+. Assuming worthlessness as the one valued commodity she had to offer was now not only useless but also contaminated, Clara retreated to her bedroom, pulled the curtains shut, shot up the last of dope and hoped to die.

The following morning, Clara stumbled into the kitchen and began rummaging through the empty, molded drawers and cabinets searching for anything to ease the pain in her hollow stomach. She found the only edible thing in the house—a partially molded yellow onion, and after carving away the fungus began to slowly chew at the harsh ration.

While sitting slouched against the cabinet, crouching on the hardwood floor, Clara's eyes aimlessly searched the room and her gaze fell upon an unrecognized object. Partly dangling from the underside of the half-open onion drawer. Clara crawled across the floor and carefully unwedged what appeared to be a gold chain. She fell back to the floor, holding the object in her hands and staring blankly, unsure of the importance of what she held.

As Clara stared she began to remember, and as she remembered she began to weep. The gold chain was holding a watch—solid 24kt gold, partially plated with alabaster, and embedded on the front of the watch was one of the rarest stones on earth—a 5 ct red diamond. While examining the watch, Clara noticed that while the hands were making movement, they were not efficiently keeping time, but were instead twitching aimlessly back and forth, the short hand dancing between the five and six, and the long between the seven and eight. Clara stared intently at the priceless trinket, as the story of the treasure she held penetrated her otherwise empty mind.

Clara's grandfather, Isaac Katz, had given her this watch the last time she saw him before he passed. Clara and Isaac had always shared a similar spirit, and while on his deathbed she was the one he asked to be alone with as he breathed his last. Clara remembered the warmth she felt that day as her grandfather drew her near. She remembered the thick smell of pipe tobacco on his breath and clothes as she buried her face in his chest while he held her head near to him. She remembered the comfort she felt as he pressed the watch into her hands, and the unexpected coolness of the metal and fine stone against her skin. Clara did not understand the gift at first, and was almost offended that someone she so cherished and revered would exit this cruel world leaving her nothing but a broken watch.

"But Grandfather," Clara questioned, "What good is an old broken watch to me?"

"Do not be deceived, my most precious child. The brokenness of a thing does not render it worthless. It is often the most broken of things, the most broken of people, that leave the biggest impact. Is this watch to be cast aside because it can no longer keep time? Should it be forgotten because its seemingly primary purpose can no longer be fulfilled? Is it not still a priceless treasure, created from the rarest and most beautiful stone in all the world? Often we think we are created for one thing, one purpose only, and if something were to come along and break us, to rob us of that purpose, then we assume there is no longer reason for our existence. Never forget, my dear Clara, what beauty there is in the broken things. Promise me you will remember this truth: there is no such thing as an invaluable thing, an invaluable person."

As Clara remembered her grandfather's words she fell into a deep stare, incapable of removing her eyes from the glare of the red jewel staring back at her, challenging her endless thought. Clara could have stayed this way eternally but was wakened from her half-slumber by a muffled roar—coming from the streets below where a growing crowd seemed to be gathering and following what looked to be a middle-aged man. Clara stumbled to the nearly shattered window and gazed outside to find a flood of people nearly drowning none other than Pope John-David. Still more than slightly dazed, Clara immediately tripped her way to the door, flung it open and stumbled down the stairs and out the door to the street below. Clara's bare feet hit the pavement just as Pope John-David and his crowd passed in front of her pathetic abode. Stunned by the scene before here, Clara stood frozen, oblivious to the scorching pavement beneath her tender feet. It was a summer day, the heat index reaching an intolerable 106 degrees, and it seemed the nearer the crowd grew the hotter Clara's entire being became. She felt her temperature rise and began to feel dizzy but was so concentrated on the crowd before her she did not begin to worry about her own well-being.

Clara stood in dazed silence and instantly snapped out of her lifeless stare when she noticed the entire crowd fall back. Where once she could not even hope to catch a glimpse of Pope John-David she now could see him clearly before her eyes. But he was not sitting, nor standing.

He was lying. On the ground. Motionless.

Clara could not comprehend what she saw before her. Why had everyone fallen back? Why was no one offering help? It seemed every soul near stood in utter shock, entirely unsure as to how to respond to such a crisis. Were they worthy to offer help? And if so, what was it he needed?

Clara fearlessly raced towards the Pope and fell at his side. When the onlookers saw it was Clara, known for her loose life-style and taboo habits, they shrank back even more. They despised her and dared not touch such a filthy human being. As Clara knelt beside the pope, the watch hung loosely around her neck and hovered over Pope John-David; and as she lowered her head and began to weep, the red diamond touched his bare chest, just where he had unbuttoned it in attempts to avoid the heat stroke that had overtaken him. The cool of the stone mixed with her flood of tears settled on his skin and trickled down his stomach, ribs and neck for endless moments until . . .

He woke.

Pope John-David's eyes opened in an instant and within seconds he rose to his feet, staring intently all the while into none but Clara's emerald eyes. He took in the sight before him, the crowd gathered, scoffing at this most wretched of persons, wondering what sort of judgment he would bestow.

But none was given.

Instead Pope John-David fell to his knees, taking both Clara's hands in his. This man, tall, broad-shouldered a spiritual and political leader giant of his time, faced this ragged mess of a human. Her oily hair sticking to a sweat-stained face, her shirt soiled and tattered, nearly see-through from wear, her hands a sticky mess.

He stared into her soul as he held her shaky hands, then took her head in his hands and drew her forehead to his lips. He held her there, then stood, and lifted her up.

"Clara," he said, with the most calm and sure voice—"All is well. Seek Truth."

Street Fight

As of late, I am frequently asked if I am okay.

It is not the shallow sort of *Are you okay?* that a co-worker asks when they see you are stressed out or that a stranger asks when you trip up the stairs at a restaurant. It is the intense, probing question that a dear friend asks when they know you are not okay at all and probably won't be for some time, but they feel obligated to ask.

My answer to this question has been, "I'm okay. I will be okay."

Do I believe that?

No I do not.

When I plead with God for peaceful sleep void of harsh dreams and fear being fully alone and in silence for even a moment—I do not believe I will be okay. When I cannot get the pain of loss out of my head and heart regardless of the time that passes by—when every other day I wonder about Life and Love and

Truth and if I'm getting it right after all—I do not necessarily *believe* I will be okay.

But I am trying.

I am trying to believe. And my active trying and intentional loving along the way—I believe is better—so much better, than plastic "faith."

We were walking the streets of downtown St. Louis. I don't remember how the conversation started or what was said that originally caused me to become so angry. But I know that at some point I said I didn't know about Jesus. In casual conversation as the three of us walked arm in arm to the The Vine (Greek restaurant) something was said to which I responded that I didn't believe that Jesus was divine and that the whole story of the crucifixion saving our souls didn't make sense.

My friend Jeremy was appalled. He was livid, in fact. What I had just said was heresy. How dare I claim the name of Christ and then utter such blasphemous words.

"It doesn't make sense to me," I said. "It just doesn't. I'm trying to believe. I would like to believe. But I don't. And the one thing I won't do is pretend to believe in something that I don't. So I am trying. And maybe one day I'll believe again. But today, I don't."

As I said, he was appalled.

Jeremy went on to give me the speech about how "That's what

faith is! It's believing, even when it doesn't make sense. It's be-lieving regardless of what you see or what makes sense."

He believed that I was wrong. Wrong for questioning. Wrong for doubting completely and fully. Wrong for altogether disbe-lieving, regardless of the fact that I am actively seeking Truth.

That's not what faith is. Not to me. Faith, to me, is not blindly believing some story because we are *supposed to*. It's not hold-ing onto a creed of beliefs because if we don't, we're going to burn in hell. It's not holding on for dear life to a belief system that doesn't make any damn sense because if we don't we are hypocritical, godless pagans.

Faith to me. . .

I don't know.

That's the point. I don't know. And that's what I said to Jeremy. I asked him, "What are you doing? What are you doing that's so right? How is your life any better than mine? You are depressed and drinking your life away and heartbroken and unhappy and claiming a religion you don't even really believe in. You just want to. You just have to. You just *must*. How does that make you any better than me? It doesn't. It makes you worse. Because while you go through life claiming Christianity and truth and all that lies therein you are living for *yourself.* You are unhappy and I am not. I am living for others. I am building homes for tornado victims and making friends with the homeless and lov-ing the broken and writing my heart out *while I doubt*. While I attempt to find Truth. I am trying to love the unlovable as

Jesus did because I *want to believe*. But I'm sure not going to pretend that I do, or that anything about Christianity makes sense because it doesn't. Not to me. Not right now."

We are scared of what we cannot control. *Not* believing in God isn't scary—believing in Him is. It means surrendering control. It means there is something bigger, more powerful than us. But it also means having Hope of something better. And Hope is not a thing to be taken lightly.

We must come to accept the reality that we cannot and will not understand all that the bible, Christianity, religion and life have to offer. And in doing so, we are giving up control. To understand, to know, is to have control. And we must come to the terrifying yet liberating realization that we do not know most things.

We were given a glimpse—we were given a Hope. And that Hope is enough. That Hope is just enough to motivate and inspire a life of compassion, intention and selfless servitude. It is enough to make us live not solely for ourselves but for the betterment of others.

It is enough to make us wonder.

CPSIA information can be obtained
at www.ICGtesting.com
Printed in the USA
FFOW04n2104230217
32788FF